LOUISE N

—

THE
ENTREPRENEURIAL
MYTH

—

A MANIFESTO FOR
REAL BUSINESS

Published by
LID Publishing Limited
The Record Hall, Studio 204,
16-16a Baldwins Gardens,
London EC1N 7RJ, UK

524 Broadway, 11th Floor, Suite 08-120,
New York, NY 10012, US

info@lidpublishing.com
www.lidpublishing.com

A member of:

BPR
Business Publishers Roundtable

www.businesspublishersroundtable.com

Printed in Great Britain by TJ International
ISBN: 978-1-912555-08-6

Cover and page design: Caroline Li

LOUISE NICOLSON

THE ENTREPRENEURIAL MYTH

A MANIFESTO FOR REAL BUSINESS

MADRID | MEXICO CITY | LONDON
NEW YORK | BUENOS AIRES
BOGOTA | SHANGHAI | NEW DELHI

DEDICATION

For Craig, Max and Oscar.

Vain are the thousand creeds
That move men's hearts, unutterably vain,
Worthless as withered weeds
Or idlest froth amid the boundless main

To waken doubt in one
Holding so fast by thy infinity,
So surely anchored on
The steadfast rock of Immortality.

With wide-embracing love
Thy spirit animates eternal years
Pervades and broods above,
Changes, sustains, dissolves, creates and rears

Extract from *No Coward Soul is Mine*
by Emily Brontë

CONTENTS

ACKNOWLEDGMENTS

Thank you, Alistair Anderson, for being the best teacher I've ever had. Thank you, Dawn Campbell, Sue Fay, Tricia Stewart and Alec Carstairs, for counsel at the beginning, middle and end of my first entrepreneurial journey. Thank you to the whole team at LID Publishing, in particular, Sara Taheri, for your support and encouragement. Thank you to the Global Women in PR management team. Thank you, James Browne and Susan McGurk, for your assistance with research. Thank you to my generous interviewees: Colin Brett, Lora Fachie, Gretchen Haskins, Dean Hunter, Bob Keiller and Colin O'Donnell.

In a twist worthy of the best stories, ten days before I filed this book's first manuscript, I was diagnosed with breast cancer; I am indebted to Marina Parton, Anna Florczak, Sarah Dyer, Karyn Shenton and every single member of the Royal Marsden and Kingston Hospital teams who work so hard to transform this brutal path into a hopeful one. I am also indebted to the friends who bore me on a tidal wave of love and prayer, kindness, humour and coaching. Thank you to the original Ardilaun gang for glorious decades served. Thank you, Bill and Matti, for the sanctuary of your love and home at thePineCone. co.uk. Thank you to the women at St Michael's Oasis, in particular, Sally, Jenny, Steph, Kate and Hanna, for being with me the night I finished this book. Thank you, Crik, for your generosity in showing me a way through with your calm example and fierce encouragement. Thank you to my brilliant girlfriends: CC, Olivia and Chrissie, Lara and Emma, Sarah and Emma, Jayne, Birgit and Amanda. Thank you, dearest Amy. Thank you, Colin. Thank you, Douglas. Thank you, Nearest and Dearest and London Friends; thank you, Coaching Gals and Oscar's Mates' Mums. You know who you are. I couldn't have done this without you. While any controversies and inaccuracies in this book are mine alone, the best bits belong to you.

To my best friend and great love, Craig, you believed I could, so I did! Thank you for your support and all we have built together. Thank you for the fun and fire of a conversation that has lasted more than 22 years. To our brilliant young men, Max and Oscar, trust grace and dare greatly because you are loved beyond measure. I can't wait to see what happens as you stride through this wonderful world.

March 2019

TAKE ANOTHER LOOK

The Entrepreneurial Myth is the exaggerated, idealized, misrepresentation of a business creator to promote widely held – but false – beliefs about enterprise, to the detriment of the individual, their business and the wider community.

You've them met before. The guy in jeans, frowning at his laptop; the woman pushing back her glasses to focus on her paper. Hunkered in a business incubator humming with entrepreneurship, they help deliver approximately £196 billion[1] to the British economy, $8.5 trillion stateside.[2]

Perhaps it's you. You trace each contour of your business in the small hours of the morning. You can still see the early breakthroughs and taste last week's mistake. The grief and the glory of small business rests in your gut. You're an entrepreneur.

Defining entrepreneurship is notoriously difficult. Many claim entrepreneurs are psychologically different, marked out from the crowd by distinct traits.[3] The label is permanent: once an entrepreneur, always an entrepreneur. Others reject this trait theory and consider entrepreneurship as an activity completed by different actors, at different times. Like basketball, entrepreneurship is a game you can start, stop, then start again later if it suits.[4] The label shifts: the player is only a player when they are standing on the court.

Research usually lumps entrepreneurs together, whatever their motivation, experience or ambition. The academic gaze often follows entrepreneurial behaviour or personality, instead of the context or values that drive activity. The economist Joseph Schumpeter suggested entrepreneurs innovate in five ways; they introduce a new good, a new method of production, create a new market or organization, or conquer a new source of raw materials. Innovation, in all its forms, is "not a feat of intellect, but of will ... a special case of the social phenomenon of leadership."[5]

But entrepreneurship is exponentially more than sweat and intellect, will and leadership. It rests on much more than innovation. With crushing logic, a businessman once claimed the only thing leaders have in common is *followers*.[6] Perhaps the only thing entrepreneurs have in common isn't innovation after all, but the creation of *opportunity*. Entrepreneurs create opportunity. Opportunity sparks hope. And you chase hope wherever it leads. This book is an opportunity to pause and contemplate where entrepreneurship ends. And it doesn't always end well.

But let's start at the beginning. The spark for this book was kindled by a master's dissertation at the University of Aberdeen nearly 20 years ago. *Modelling the Evolution of Entrepreneurial Mythology*[7] examined how journalists and a newspaper-loving public created vivid entrepreneurial caricatures in the pages of national broadsheets. Male entrepreneurs – and they were nearly always men – were portrayed as wolfish charmers, supernatural gurus, saviours, corruptors and skyrockets. Two media samples were compared; the first in 1989 and the second in 2000. Between the two samples, heroic entrepreneurs were portrayed with increasingly fantastical superpowers and steadily grew in political influence. As the entrepreneurial ego surged forward, the uncritical public adoration recorded in 1989 gave way to irritation by 2000. The gap between the idolatry of business creation and the gritty reality of entrepreneurship grew. In this gap, the entrepreneur's psyche suffered: it is impossible to be god and (business)man at the same time. The thesis closed by predicting a new post-entrepreneurial age in which entrepreneurship could be reinvented for the benefit of all. It was an audacious conclusion: 2000 was a year weighted with worship of businessmen as they gulped champagne with celebrities and loudly advised politicians how best to save the world. Nevertheless, the dissertation earnt full marks from Aberdeen University's Centre of Entrepreneurship and was featured in a special edition of the academic journal *Entrepreneurship Theory and Practice*.[8] The much-cited article was co-authored with Distinguished Professor Alistair R Anderson; you'll meet him again in Chapter 15 as he reflects on a return of the research he originally supervised in 2001.

After the master's degree, life resumed with marriage, sons and friends; with work in journalism and public relations (PR); with the expectant launch and painful sale of a consultancy business. The Entrepreneurial Myth hummed throughout. It underscored the business features commissioned by editors. It was the drumbeat of numerous PR campaigns created to launch client adventures and build public personalities. It was the metronome to seven years as an entrepreneur in the creative industries. A PR knows stories matter. And if a story sticks, for decades, it should eventually be tested, told and trusted.

So, in the summer of 2018, the master's research was carefully repeated. Instead of pouring over newspaper articles preserved on royal blue microfiche film in the library, evidence was comfortably gathered by Google. In total, over 1,000 media articles were sampled from a 30-year period, and 50 years of UK, US, Chinese and Indian enterprise policy was interrogated and analysed. All this proved that entrepreneurs are still promoted and pursued as modern Greek gods. This isn't a harmless cartoon-ish characterization. The gap between the entrepreneur of myth and reality has damaging consequences for business creators, their communities and economies. The Myth's insidious toxicity had simmered and intensified over the past 30 years; people still suffer today because of its exaggerations, distortions and lies.

It's time to change. This book, which originated in the university library and has been enriched by corporate decades, is now in your hands. It is an invitation to help break The Entrepreneurial Myth's momentum; to help rebuild a more reflective, more effective entrepreneurship for the health and wealth of all. The wellbeing of brilliant entrepreneurial minds and the wealth of global economies depend on it.

This is a love letter to entrepreneurship; a heartfelt intervention by an author who has studied, launched, grown, sold, joined and promoted entrepreneurial businesses for decades. The mission is to recalibrate entrepreneurship so that it works better. The criticism is directed to the distorted image of entrepreneurship in popular culture – the Myth – not towards the vital human drive to create and trade. Entrepreneurship has the power to energize communities, fuel nations and, literally, change the world. There is a unique pinch of pleasure to be found in creating a business from scratch. Sometimes the satisfaction is profound and takes you by surprise. It's the keys to a new office; the blur of an evening at an industry awards party; the spike of adrenaline on hearing that a client wants you. But there are already numerous books, articles, podcasts and shows offering entrepreneurial romance.

The urgent, unexamined, problem is that society's hunger for entrepreneurship's mythical promise, plus an ancient craving for heroic stories, distorts how businesses are perceived, created, delivered and supported. This distortion damages entrepreneurs and the economies they serve. And there is a different way.

So, take another look. Compare the entrepreneur promoted through business schools, economic policy and your newspaper, with the real-life, first-person experience of running a small business. The Entrepreneur strides through the daily news as an all-powerful, never-fail guru.

His personality fizzes with energy; he's bold, creative, comfortable with risk and uncertainty. He's larger than life; a time traveller; an economic saviour. He is courted by politicians as the personification of a healthy, dynamic economy. The Entrepreneur creates jobs and drives growth. The deliberate male pronoun jars, but the Myth is doggedly and unapologetically male. You know the names of The Entrepreneurs; Richard and Steve, Elon and Jack. They need little introduction.

In stark contrast, the entrepreneur at the heart of real business is just a man or a woman. Let's say it's you. Invisible to most, you shoulder the gruelling hard work and gnawing anxieties of small business. You drink warm white wine at networking events. You accept responsibility for your workplace family, to the detriment of your own. The vertigo of a successful month still sparks anxiety.

One bears little relation to the other. There is a yawning gap between the mythical Entrepreneur promoted through education, politics and media – and the messy, fallible, real thing. This gap – The Entrepreneurial Myth – damages people by isolating, stressing and exiling real business creators. Consider the collateral damage to entrepreneurial mental health: entrepreneurs are significantly more likely to present mental health concerns than a member of the general population.[9] This must change.

The Entrepreneurial Myth also damages our economies and societies as it persuades the public and politicians to accept, even celebrate, appalling business failure rates. Essential business talent is excluded and attitudes to success and failure distorted. All this is to the detriment of our economy. Name another economic sector which potentially receives more government funding than essential

emergency services, without providing the jobs or innovation to justify that support,[10] and stubbornly boasts a 90%
failure rate. This, too, must change.

This book's purpose is to deconstruct The Entrepreneurial Myth and strip it of its power to damage business creators
and the economies they serve. You need to see it, and understand it, to change it. Then, a more reflective, more effective,
form of entrepreneurship is proposed for the health and
wealth of all. We need entrepreneurship but we also need to
look after the people that drive it. A revolution rests on the
fact that a more reflective entrepreneurship is a more effective entrepreneurship. Rarely can you have it all, yet nurturing entrepreneurial mental health also nurtures economic
productivity; it circumvents the breath-taking waste of failed
businesses. This is not a soft option; it's the smart option.

Three pillars prop up the analysis: first, the ancient history of storytelling, myth and metaphor explains why we
deify entrepreneurs. Second, social psychology explores the
personal impact of The Entrepreneurial Myth on individual business creators. Third, economics explores the costly
economic exchange society makes for the inefficiencies of
The Entrepreneurial Myth.

Change will come. Entrepreneur is an almost ubiquitous
job title. Entrepreneurial business birth rates increase year on
year, as do business death rates.[11] This start-up churn creates
and takes jobs; it demands blood and sweat, tears and generates eye-watering transaction costs in an imperfect market.
Imagine the prize if the churn was steadied and reduced.
Back of the envelope calculations show that if business success rates improved by just 10%, it could be worth £19.6 billion
to the UK economy; $850 billion to the US economy. Detailed
financial analysis will follow, but whatever the financial

advantage of unpicking the Myth to create enterprise fit for the next generation, it is coupled with the urgent, unquantifiable human benefit of preserving the mental health and well-being of entrepreneurs and their families.

Imagine seeing entrepreneurs as they really are. Just men and women with a patchwork of skills and a fallible flash of brilliance. Like you, like me; not God, guru or superman. Closing the gap between the mythological entrepreneurship peddled in public, and the real thing, changes how entrepreneurs are supported and how businesses are built. It changes how failure is managed and success is celebrated.

This is a global issue. As economies converge, we need a shared understanding about enterprise and its protagonists. Consequently, this book considers the impact of The Entrepreneurial Myth in the UK and the US, India and China. Norms, aspirations and business practices merge as the 88% of the world's population who live outside the West seek the living standards, (relative) peace and prosperity that most Western citizens have enjoyed over the past few decades.[12] Countries with radically different cultures pursue the same entrepreneurial ideals to drive their economy towards prosperity. Entrepreneurship blends values, ideas, models, money and markets in a way that accelerates globalization. The Entrepreneurial Myth bridges cultures and countries, sectors and decades; a broad global perspective is absolutely essential.

You are invited to speak, reflect, connect, learn and persist in a movement to preserve the best of real entrepreneurial business. Pick up a pen, scrawl in the margin, join the discussion online and make the Real Business Manifesto yours.

Now turn to the first of three pillars in Part 1 – history – to consider the ancient history of storytelling, myth and metaphor and understand why we deify entrepreneurs.

PART 1.

HISTORY.
WHAT HAS BEEN WILL BE AGAIN

CHAPTER 1.
MAPPING MEANING

Look up from this book and peel back the corners of the scene in front of you. Look underneath. Each person you see fizzes with 1,000 trillion synapses, will utter 16,000 words[13] and make up to 35,000 choices before the end of the day. Data and opportunity combine in a tangle of overwhelming complexity.

To function, you need a map. This map can be the grammar shaping your speech, a habit determining your schedule or the cultural expectations salting your future. It can be anything that sorts and tidies. A map organizes life's beautiful chaos into something that you can live with.

Meaning comes from the map, not the territory it depicts. You are not the sum of your sensory data. Instead, culture and cognition, emotion and experience, act as filters actively shaping reality. If there is no such thing as a pure experience or even a truly factual recall of that experience, "we are all our own metaphysicians, even if we are not usually aware of it."[14] Imagine that!

This is essentially a constructionist perspective – a field of psychology and sociology that reveals the socially constructed nature of society and reality. It explains how words make worlds[15] and how your brain generates experience. The assumption is that the physical world is weak and constructionism is the cradle that supports your experience.[16] For now, consider the use of maps, or 'schema' if you want the technical word, to parcel and make sense of a messy world. You create most of the unique world that you experience.

Yet no man is an island. Humans crave connection with others. You are driven to make meaning and share meaning. Do you *really* know what I mean?

Maps are informed by politics, economics, psychology and law – yet feel intensely personal. Every one of the 7.6 billion people alive develops mental maps through trial and error, bitter experience and occasional reflection. Maps are made in isolation, by one author, set in one time and place and generation. The generation in which the map-reader sits believes it is utterly unique: more intelligent than those it follows, wiser than those it leads. This is a folly that means each generation repeats numerous cognitive lessons.

But mental maps are shared. The production and circulation of meaning in all forms is an academic field called semiology.[17] Think of semiology like coding. Create your message; weigh it in your hand to test its meaning; guess its impact; launch it through the air. The message, once caught and decoded, might be understood. A reply is crafted and returned. This means there is no such thing as a 'raw' historical event. Events are transformed by this encoding and decoding process used to communicate them.

Life events have to become a 'story' to be communicated and shared.[18]

Consequently, humans are innate storytellers who organize thoughts into narratives.[19] You don't appraise a message received on its own merits; instead, you check how it fits with the stories you already believe. You edit the story to fit your bias. You add your own flourish before you reply. You can't help it; stories are an unconscious psychological impulse. This is why stories intuitively satisfy. Think of the gentle balance of a poem or the comfort of one more bedtime tale. It's easier to recall stories than facts; stories *make sense* of facts.

Establishing the story shared between sender and receiver is notoriously difficult. The relationship between what is meant, said and understood can be arbitrary. Language is inadequate. Meaning hangs in the tension between words and underscores words not used. Language doesn't just label thoughts; it creates, changes or hides thoughts.[20]

Metaphor helps; verbal pictures carry meaning that is otherwise difficult to articulate. Metaphor eloquently communicates complexity, like vivid illustrations in a storybook. This colourful packaging ensures myths and stories stick in the mind and are gleefully passed on.

But now hear the clatter of competing messages and media noise that sabotages your message as it travels from one person to another. Now speed up the coding and decoding of communication; perhaps multiply it by the 269 billion daily emails exchanged[21] and never switch it off. Add more semiotic messages through the food you eat, the clothes you wear and the music you download. Stories are often spoken or written, of course, but the field of

semiology reminds us of how rich and layered and complex communication can be. Your boss' sequin shirt is a
story. The fake grass in reception is a story. The Friday box
of doughnuts may be a minor character in your corporate
story but still speaks volumes. Everything you do, or don't
do, says something.

Despite these complications, we connect. Think of the
deep pleasure of joining a cause which inspires you to raise
your voice or fist in unison. Think of one of those late-night
conversations plotting a new landscape. Think of the last
time you felt understood. These imperfect, exhilarating
moments of pouring over a shared map are memorable
because they are rare. It is like hearing your hometown
accent when sat in a café, 3,000 miles from family. You recognize the voice and it connects you to something larger
than the coffee on the table in front of you. These shared
moments – or collective maps – reveal what really matters
to you and what you really need to thrive.

CHAPTER 2.
TELL ME A STORY

Stories are essential collective maps which package your experience in a digestible form. Stories are the backbone of history. They are the pulsing 24-hour headline on your phone. They sustain case law and corporate life.

Newspapers deliver stories. They are a convenient daily record of the myth and metaphor we use to understand and construct the world around us. Journalists are the preeminent storytellers of modern society. An editor's authorized version of the news is a convenient daily record of what a community values and fears. It is cultural short-hand for a society's perceptions and assumptions. And it's significantly easier to sample than the worlds we create verbally at the watercooler.

This is why this book analysed newspapers to access psychological and cultural perceptions of entrepreneurs and their businesses.

From a social constructionist perspective, the black and white print of a newspaper is a mental map. The map reveals how the journalist, editor and reader make sense of a chaotic world. What is written, what is left out, the edit and tone, the position on the page and the photo – all tell us something about the writer and the subject and the world they live in. News is not an inert mirror pursuing truth and reflecting reality. It's much more important than that. Through an unavoidably selective and biased process, newspapers inform the reader what is notable in the first place. This is often with dramatic effect. As the French playwright Jean Anouilh asked: "have you noticed that life, real honest-to-goodness life, with murders and catastrophes and fabulous inheritances, happens almost exclusively in the newspapers?" Instead of passively reflecting who we are and what we value, media content shapes and changes our world around us. Good journalism *creates* popular culture.[22]

While smitten with print, this book defines 'newspaper' in the broadest possible sense. 'Newspaper' includes media through television, podcasts, publishing and ads. While ancient myths were predominantly shared through oral tradition, today, ink and code transmit new translations of archetypal stories. Whatever the semiotic process, sampling methodology or media, The Entrepreneurial Myth has endured for decades. Park your loyalty to one paper over another. When you consider how The Entrepreneurial Myth saturates one broadsheet over a 30-year period, you will view business discourse afresh. You will see proof of the Myth and its impact everywhere.

Don't be deceived. Not every story is good for us. "Communication can be informative even if it's not true," the brilliant Evan Davis reminds us.[23] "It can be persuasive even if it is not informative; it can be effective in the short term even if it is not persuasive in the long term.

And if everyone is doing it, it can be irresistible even if it is not effective." Maps are essential to decipher a messy world stuffed with data and opportunity but one particular map – The Entrepreneurial Myth – damages individuals, businesses, communities and economies.

Shared stories fuel The Entrepreneurial Myth by drawing a line from ancient heroes to today's business protagonist. The map handed down to entrepreneurs turns the chaos of regular business into a clean path: *Eureka!* Funding. Growth. Success. Sales. This narrative can make you sick. It skews definitions and expectations of success and failure. This entrepreneurial map skews public policy, challenges entrepreneurs' mental health, potentially amplifies business failure rates and undermines our economies. Initial research[24] reveals that over 49% of sampled entrepreneurs have one or more mental health conditions, compared with 32% of the research study's non-entrepreneurial control group. And still, up to 90% of entrepreneurial businesses will fail despite record levels of investment. The price is high, while the prize is uncertain.

However, if you understand how maps work, you can draw a different line. You can edit the business landscape to reframe success and well-being at work. The pen in your hand can draw a more reflective, more effective entrepreneurship. This new line – the Real Business Manifesto – is proposed later. But before you turn cartographer, let's dissect The Entrepreneurial Myth's inheritance.

CHAPTER 3.
STORY AUTOPSY

German ethnologist Adolf Bastian observed that myths and folk tales followed *elementargedenken* or 'elemental ideas'. Sigmund Freud drew parallels between dreams and the scripts of folk tales. He believed that myth packages powerful unconscious fears and desires in a manageable way. Stories and dreams are ultimately an outlet for ideas you would normally repress and bury. Carl Jung believed in a universal psychological inheritance to accompany genetic inheritance. These ancestral 'archetypes' or 'primordial images' symbolize basic human motivations, values and personalities – they shape the human psyche.

Think of personal narratives like layers of sedimentary rock. Stand back to see the coloured stripes of collective stories that form with time. The human brain loves patterns; it is inherently lazy and chooses the most energy efficient path.[25] The story you have heard before shapes the story you tell. Humans form herds.[26] The story you hear from others shapes the story you live. There is a direct relationship between the narratives you create internally to make sense of a messy, data-packed world, and collective stories shared by members of the same culture, community or industry.

Consequently, familiar characters populate shared stories: the hero ready to rescue; the old man with a spark in his eye and a wise word; the trickster and the trouble-maker. All can be found in Jung's archetypes. But while others hint at the characters, stories and maps we share, only British journalist Christopher Booker knits it together to reveal the treasure of a hidden, universal language in his book *The Seven Basic Plots*.[27] Booker's epic anthropological study of common stories identifies seven universal plots: defeating the monster, comedy, tragedy and rebirth, rags to riches, the quest, voyage and return.

The monster plot involves an all-powerful hero, armed with magic weapons, who fights a monster and cheats death. Consider the labours of Heracles, which involved a golden lion, man-eating birds and a nine-headed Hydra. It's not just the Greeks. The Norse sagas, Germanic and Celtic epics also conjured terrifying monsters. These monsters represent the worst fears of an egocentric human nature. Their furious egos cloud their judgement, so the hero ultimately outwits the monster to claim the treasure.

The second plot is comedy, the third is tragedy. In a comedy, confusion and misunderstanding prevail. The story is a mess that needs sorting; a puzzle that needs solving. Just before irrevocable damage, the dark figures repent, identities are revealed, division and loss are repaired. There is a lightness of touch: phew, it is all alright in the end! But if the story doesn't end in love and relief, you have comedy's dark twin, tragedy. The hero is frustrated, dissatisfied and out of control. Their mind is divided; their relationships destroyed.

They are caught in their own quandary and the only ending is death. Compare Shakespearean comedy *As You Like It* with the tragedy *Macbeth*.

In the rebirth plot, the hero is subdued by poison or a spell and suffers physical isolation or spiritual imprisonment. The wintery state can be broken, just in the nick of time, if the hero is liberated by love. *Sleeping Beauty* is the classic story archetype illustrating Booker's rebirth plot.

Of course, a business doesn't fight a real monster and rarely ends in gruesome tragedy. The remaining universal plots chime with today's entrepreneurial journey. This time imagine the hero in a trouser suit ...

The quest plot involves a hero's long, perilous journey to a distant land for something of infinite value. They are urgently called away from home. The wild terrain, inevitable tribulations and temptations don't deter them. They are not alone; their companions complete them and support them. They are helped by a wise old man or young maiden who selflessly makes the ultimate sacrifice for their hero's triumphant liberation. Think *Jason and the Argonauts* or *The Lord of the Rings*. Think of Virgin Group's quest to and "go into markets where others dare not tread ... to create new world-changing experiences" and "test the boundaries of human capabilities and technologies."[28]

Now consider voyage and return. Our hero travels from normal life to a brave new world bloated with freaks and marvels. There is always trouble and a thrilling escape back to the safety of home. Only now the hero has a different perspective. Remember *Alice in Wonderland* or the *The Wizard of Oz*? Hear the voyage myth at the heart of Jack Ma's marriage: "In Ying's eyes, Jack was a ship. She had built their home into a harbour where Jack's ship would come for fresh water and supplies before inevitably setting off on the next voyage."[29]

Perhaps the never-ending challenges of a quest or voyage are the root of today's business failure fetish. Failure fetish is the manic urge to fail faster, embrace failure, even enjoy it. Jason and Hercules stuck to the script and struggled on. Chapter Seven returns to this theme and explores attitudes to failure in much more detail. For now, perhaps you can hear the Greek heroes' tenacity in Instagram encouragement to never give up in your modern business quest for treasure.

Last, but perhaps the most important script for entrepreneurs, is the rags to riches plot. The hero is ordinary and insignificant, scorned and ignored. They are dominated by egotistical and deceitful characters. Perhaps you know them already? They step onto the stage and are suddenly, deservedly, revealed as exceptional. Material circumstances have improved beyond their wildest dreams, but the wealth is symbolic. Riches illustrate an inward transformation as the hero grows up and discovers their true self. Importantly, the hero now has a kingdom and inheritance over which they can rule. They have passed the test and order has been restored. This plot is the ultimate universal tale and can be traced throughout Europe, Africa, Asia, North America and China. Clark Kent really started out as a ninth-century Cinderella.

Rags to riches is a plot that runs like an underground river through numerous real entrepreneurial life stories. From Aristotle's *Poetics*, failure and success are conceptualized as opposite spokes of a wheel moving imperceptibly, inevitably, round and round and round. To this day, Aristotle shapes attitudes to risk and reward. You anxiously assume the heady days of celebrity and fortune will 'turn down' to disaster. While the successful business protagonist balances at the top, with political and media audiences looking on in awe, deep down he suffers vertigo, afraid of the inevitable fall. For some, it manifests as the psychological phenomenon Imposter Syndrome – the insidious belief that, despite evidence of skills and success, you remain a fraud. The reality is that business is messy. The daily maelstrom of operational decisions, offhand comments and human fallibility pull the business protagonist down. With feet of clay, and an unforgiving audience, no-one remains on top forever. Alternatively, we anticipate hard-won reward when at the bottom. Peripety reassures us that everything will be alright in the end. The plots we read and live by run deep. They overlap and build on one another.

STILL I RISE

All seven plots share a hero, somehow incomplete, who is summoned by a call to adventure. There is usually a perilous path peppered with existential challenges and thrilling near-death escapes. The hero tenaciously rises as the plot pulses between dark confrontations and liberating triumphs. The happy ending reflects a new cosmic balance, while the hubris and fatal flaw of the hero sabotages our catharsis. These themes inform the business worlds we build and inhabit today.

CHAPTER 4.
MODERN GREEK GODS

Ultimately the universal plots – particularly quest, voyage and rags to riches – illuminate scripts followed by modern entrepreneurs. Here is the evidence.

The **bold words** throughout this book are plucked straight from the pages of newspapers sampled over the past 30 years. No poetic licence is necessary: these bold words are reproduced exactly as they appeared in your daily read in 1989, 2001 and 2017/18. Can you hear the seven plots? Listen how this language builds an exaggerated ideal of the Herculean entrepreneur.

An apology before you begin: male pronouns rightly provoke feminist indignation but are deliberate here and as they appear in the newspapers' entrepreneurial stories. The gendered impact of the male Entrepreneurial Myth is dissected in Chapter Five.

That's magic. As early as 1989, entrepreneurs are described in the daily news as the supernatural **magician at the heart of it all**, with **near magical powers** and the ability to **cast a spell and make it all alright**. Founder of

Cowboy Ventures, Aileen Lee, recently coined the term **unicorn** for any tech start-up that reaches a billion-dollar value. The fantastical label has captured commentators' imagination who embellish stories with descriptions of the **shiniest horns** and **cleanest hooves**. The BBC's reality show where entrepreneurs pitch for cash, **Dragon's Den**, played with similar metaphors of Herculean beasts and pitches going **up in smoke**. Magical imagery surges through the 30-year sample with frequent references to **conjuring** and **bewitchment**. Entrepreneurs are portrayed as **sprinkling magic dust** on businesses, **producing ideas and concepts like a magician might fling confetti out of a top hat** in a **mysterious modern form of alchemy**.

Larger than life. Media descriptions of entrepreneurs distort their scale and influence. Throughout the 30-year sample, and particularly in the noughties, entrepreneurs are described with **giant hands**, or **giant boots**, **sitting on top of companies**, **stalking Wall Street**. Occasionally they turn ferocious **giant killer** to battle other **market giants**. Britain becomes little more than the **giant's theme park for ... entrepreneurs to plunder**. Business protagonists take the **secret magic sauce** to become **Goliath, Gandalf** or a **titan of the internet**.

Time traveller. The **ubiquitous entrepreneur** bends time with his **epic ability to bridge the centuries-wide gap between different countries**. He is on **top of the world**, at the **crossroads of humanity** or in a **galaxy of would-be predators**. The entrepreneur is accused of **over-reaching reality**, located where the **future has already happened**. His **visceral urge to control destiny** is celebrated. The supernatural impact of entrepreneurship creates **a new order of things** as a metaphorical **storm rages**. Sometimes, the entrepreneur scares himself by **opening Pandora's box** and sharing a **dystopian vision leading to wars and maybe even the apocalypse.** His quest involves **the thrill, dread and sleepless nights that come with being an entrepreneur.** Rest assured, he'll eventually **triumph over crushed fingers** and markets with a **wolfish smile.** And when order is restored, he'll enjoy **bizarre Twitter rants** about who might become the **ruler of the world.**

Stanger than fiction. At least one entrepreneur is rumoured to have inspired a superhero's foil as **real-life Tony Stark.** You can meet his peers as **Welsh wizard, pirate, Marlboro man, Aztec chieftain, iconic legend** or **master of the universe.** In a spectacular piece of modern media mythology, Richard Branson is granted supernatural powers as a **bearded shadow … hovering over the market.** Features paint the entrepreneur as **Darth Vader,** or the **sun king,** or **Peter Pan,** working as a **whirlwind,** in the **labyrinth, striving to take away the poison** to create the **blinding glow** of profit. There is striking quest and rebirth imagery in today's newspaper coverage of entrepreneurial businesses.

God complex. At the beginning of the 30-year sample, the entrepreneur might have been described as **blessed with resources** or **God-given opportunities.** By the noughties, he is described as God himself. He is a **priest architect, guru, godhead of an extraordinary network of power** or, in one brilliantly underplayed commentary, **at least like the Archbishop of Canterbury. Disciples, followers** and **fervent believers in product** are urged to put their **faith** in the entrepreneur's **parable** and

build Jerusalem. The entrepreneur is granted power to **answer prayers, evangelize, prophesise,** even **defy original sin.** Business people create **temples of endeavour,** a **new artistic Eden, peace in heaven** or the **reincarnation of economic policy.** The entrepreneur is a **technological missionary** madly pursing the **Holy Grail.** Biblical weight is given to an entrepreneur's decision to return to Britain: the **land of free enterprise calls back lost prodigal sons.** The Entrepreneurial Myth builds **impossible fantasies of world domination,** a **brave new world** and a **masterplan for life.** The entrepreneur is an **untouchable demi-god** who needs worship. The audience is happy to oblige and obediently sit at leaders' feet for **ten top tips to achieve insane success.**

Romance isn't dead. There is palpable romance in newspaper rags to riches stories. Meet **a pillow salesman** who turned an **idea plucked from a dream into a successful international business claiming nearly 30 million sales.** Or a **quintessentially American wild ride from pig farms to the gold-plated halls of Mar-a-Lago.** Or the business that **started in a broom cupboard at the back of an office in Portobello Road but sold for £577million.** Or the woman who **made watches for 75p per day** but now strides **the path to huge success.** Pick up today's paper for the latest example of this damaging entrepreneurial shorthand. The journey described deletes real business struggles.

Money from stones. The entrepreneur **always charms.** The guru entrepreneur **combines scholarship with the ability to charm funding from stones.** He knows **how to charm a waitress into serving cherry pie when the menu says apple.** These business protagonists are **elegant and subtle subversive**s, credited with **flair**, **spark**, or a **magnetic personality**. Although the journalist is not always seduced by the entrepreneur's **glitz cults**, **lustre and hype**, the stereotype of the **engaging eccentric English** entrepreneur perseveres. The agency and pace of the business maverick gathers pace through the noughties. The **charming maniac** is defined by his **nervy, exhilarating** energy. He is charged with providing **a glint of glamour in an otherwise dull but solid business**. By 2018, the entrepreneur is depicted as out of control. **Crazy Bob the entrepreneur** manically **hacks bio-chemistry, loads the silliest thing imaginable onto a rocket** or designs brand names that can be sang to Beethoven's Fifth Symphony.

BETWEEN THE LINES

This entrepreneurial mythology is not mere journalistic licence or editorial narrative. The potency of imagery ricocheting from ancient myth to your daily newspaper – and the world it creates in your mind – cannot be underestimated. If the guru entrepreneur is an all-powerful magician, distorting time and space like God, you unwittingly hold stratospheric expectations of the business protagonist in front of you. If they are depicted as a charming eccentric on an inevitable climb to riches, perhaps it's harder to believe business success is possible for people like you.

This is the essence of The Entrepreneurial Myth: the exaggerated, relentless misrepresentation of business protagonists to peddle false beliefs about enterprise. It misleads our political discourse. It distorts business and trade policy.

Perhaps most importantly, the Myth profoundly impacts entrepreneurs themselves to the detriment of their businesses, communities and economies.

IN BRIEF:
HISTORY

- By dipping into psychology and sociology, this book reveals how our language, communication, culture and emotion shapes our understanding and experience of reality; this is called a social constructionist perspective. It also draws on a field of social psychology called semiotics.
- We create and rely on psychological 'maps' to make sense of overwhelming amounts of external data. Humans are innately social beings, so we share these mental maps, and create collective maps, in order to understand each other.
- Language can be an inadequate means of sharing understanding, so we use metaphor as a way of communicating things that it is otherwise difficult to articulate. This is why we love stories; they help make sense of our reality and communicate our understanding.
- Newspapers deliver stories and construct culture. Newspapers were picked as a handy daily semiotic record of our understanding of businesses and the

people who run them. This book rests on analysis of a 30-year sample of the ways in which entrepreneurs are portrayed in the news.

- Analysis of the news reveals entrepreneurs are positioned as the new Greek gods; ancient universal plots of monsters, rag-to-riches, quests and voyages vividly colour our communication about entrepreneurs and their businesses.
- The Entrepreneurial Myth damages individual entrepreneurs, their communities and economies.

Three pillars underpin this book. You have considered the first pillar, history. Now turn to the second pillar in Part Two – psychology – to explore the personal impact of The Entrepreneurial Myth on individual business creators.

PART 2.

PSYCHOLOGY.
ME, MY HEALTH AND I

CHAPTER 5.
TALENT EXCLUDED

The Entrepreneurial Myth excludes talent from real business; it insists that the entrepreneur is an exceptional person with limitless ideas and magical resources. Their guts hold the answer. As The Entrepreneurial Myth gains momentum, being entrepreneurial is increasingly considered the norm. There is a millennial insistence that 'we are all entrepreneurs now'. One blogger/author describes an entrepreneur as **anyone sat at their kitchen table with an idea ... If you have a smartphone or a laptop and an idea, you can be entrepreneurial**, she claims. Another contributor insists being entrepreneurial is about the **innate ability to survive because survival involves innovative thinking**. Of course, start-up statistics infer *losing*, not surviving, is all it takes to be entrepreneurial. There is undoubtedly something wrong with the term entrepreneur. It has become so bloated with different characteristics that it can be used to describe everyone.

In contrast, The Entrepreneurial Myth is very specific. The Entrepreneurial Myth doesn't portray every man or woman as entrepreneurial. It repeatedly shines the spotlight of thousands of stories, evidenced in a 30-year media sample, on the protagonist on stage: they are special, they have all the ideas and all the answers. They are the hero defeating a dragon, a shark, perhaps even a unicorn. While The Entrepreneurial Myth relentlessly taps into ancient plots and dominates public debate about enterprise, the modern audience's claim to be an 'entrepreneur too' is, for now, just heckling.

The Myth's insistence that the entrepreneur is special means they are not 'one of us'. This otherness creates a false barrier. People who don't conform to the entrepreneurial stereotype of the thrusting white man are excluded. Money follows the Myth as private equity and venture capital investments tend to favour the same demographic. The UK Business Angels Association revealed ingrained societal assumptions that small and medium-sized enterprise (SME) investment is the preserve of ultra-wealthy, white, male Londoners. All female teams were awarded $1.9 billion – just 2.2% – of the $85 billion total invested by venture capitalists.[30] Despite making up 51% of the population, women currently own only 17% of UK SMEs.[31] Are you angry yet? Black, Asian and other ethnic minority groups in the UK are underrepresented in entrepreneurial statistics; 5% of the UK's small businesses are led by someone from an ethnic minority group, while 90% of small businesses are led by a white business owner. This is despite the fact that gender diverse companies outperform their less diverse peers by 15%, while more racially diverse teams outperform their peers by 35%.[32] It seems that The Entrepreneurial Myth maintains privilege by excluding talent desperately needed by real business.

THE MYTH IS MALE

Entrepreneurs are portrayed as societal outsiders who break the rules and plot a different path. Within entre-preneurial ranks, women remain outsiders. The frequent prefix, *female* entrepreneur, or new saccharine words like fempreneur or mumpreneur, prove that The Entre-preneurial Myth is exclusive and male. Modified names, softer somehow and often printed in pink ink, betray the assumption that entrepreneurship isn't for women or at least looks radically different.

Consider evidence from the 30-year media sample that underpins this book. The first media sample in 1989 revealed just one in 240 articles featured a female entre-preneur. She was a **new breed of erotica enthusiast**, alleg-edly **emancipated beyond feminism**, harassing men with engravings of naked women. In 2000, the second sample of 240 articles held only 12 articles featuring women entre-preneurs. These articles profiled her familial relationships or feelings, not the shape and statistics of her business. Consider this: **she's entrepreneur of the year [and] also a devoted mother dedicated to her family. She has back up from her husband, who works part-time, proving that these days behind every great woman is a great man**. Eighteen years on and, while the language may be more self-conscious, the message is the same. Women remain defined by their relationships in a way men aren't. Meet **two working mums** with the **billionaire boyfriend** or **famous father**. For many women, explains one article, **children are their side hustle**. An entrepreneur chips in, **I didn't have a boyfriend for a whole year and no man wants to put up with a woman who has 17 seconds to spare on a Saturday evening**. The businesses featured in 2018 media are anchored in the female sphere: repackaging tampons in ice cream tubs, lingerie and plus-size clothing to empower, lipstick collaborations, a polygamous dating app and breastmilk banks. **The year of the women-led period start-up!** declared Forbes. If women enter a male-dominated space, they meet **Silicon Valley's white bro culture** or **grim sexual harassment**. A business feature describes a formidable magic circle lawyer as **defeated by her tight waistband on long-haul flights.** Another 2018 article describes women as **the rarer sex when it comes to wealth creation**. Women are **better at crowdfunding**, concedes a different writer, but still **too conservative to scale** venture capital-backed businesses. Business women define themselves through their relationships. Unlike men interviewed, she describes the career bursts between pregnancies or namechecks the mentor who opened the door. **People think my husband is giving me money for a hobby to keep me quiet at home,** laughs one entrepreneur. The journalist pushes back this time: **this is a business built on more than pocket money**.

Research[33] consistently proves there are more similarities than differences in entrepreneurial motivation between the sexes. That said, the overdue rallying cry of 'men, women, equal, different'[34] gains deserved ground. There is some evidence that women may be creating new schema for themselves. Alternative mental maps include ditching the term entrepreneur altogether: women prefer founder, owner, even multi-hyphenate. The problem remains that money, resources and support are wired to serve the word entrepreneurship. In a recent study,[35] women demonstrated stronger ambition and higher profits than their male counterparts but attracted less funding and experienced more discrimination. Those who don't fit the entrepreneurial stereotype are excluded. This is an irritant and injustice for women who lead. It also damages economic health and wealth. Imagine the difference it would make if women-led businesses accessed more than their allotted 2.2% of venture capital dollars.[36] What do you want an entrepreneur to look like anyway?

CHAPTER 6.
WEAKNESS DEMONIZED

The Entrepreneurial Myth demonizes weakness. If a business falters, public opinion stalks spooked chief executives. The Greek chorus is relentlessly vitriolic. While The Entrepreneurial Myth isolates business protagonists as they rise on Aristotle's wheel, it ruthlessly exiles those who fail. Some hasten the end to entrepreneurial isolation with tabloid-worthy sabotage – perhaps the classic egotistical workplace affair. Others distract observers with desperate turnaround plans.

The Entrepreneurial Myth isolates and exiles with the lie that the answer to business success is deep inside: the burden for economic success is placed on entrepreneurs' shoulders *and* buried in his guts. This is a colossal waste of business time, money and resources. However gleefully business creators climb up the pedestal to collude with the Myth, the inevitable fall is bad for businesses, economies and communities. The media maps this damage: you'll have heard The Entrepreneurial Myth's sneer before. Again, **bold words** are direct quotes from a media sample spanning three decades.

A TIRED MAN AND A BAD DAY

Turn back to your daily read and enterprise culture is charged with **aggravating misery for profit** sparking **social chaos**, the **ruinous state of the family** and **the human wreckage that fills the doctors' surgeries, psychiatric wards and mailbags of advice columnists**. As the newspapers rattle into 2000, the entrepreneurial guru is unpicked and critiqued. An entrepreneur's human weakness can be found as The Entrepreneurial Myth is exposed. While supernatural imagery dominates, a distinct undercurrent of media stories charts the entrepreneur's unavoidable human characteristics. Entrepreneurs are described as **struggling, greedy, neurotic** or **stupid**. Consider the brilliant headline from year 2000, **Gates Knackered**. And 18 years on, with the same sigh, **Zuckerberg is not having a great week**. Imagine that: a tired human and a bad day. Stories become increasingly ferocious through the 30-year media sample. Reverence is dashed. Entrepreneurs are described as **depressed** and **lonely, broken** and **addicted**. "**Anybody who says they are a guru is probably history**," agrees one. Others, fight. **Scammers, mercenaries** and **pirates** rage about **acrimonious disputes**. There is **fraud, suicide** and **alienation** as Schumpeterian entrepreneurs are publicly accused of having **moved too fast and broken too many things**.

Yet, despite all this, entrepreneurial pain remains a minor character in business stories. The public narrative quickly returns to more comfortable territories of quest, treasure and triumph. The Myth likes to have it both ways: entrepreneurs are heroic gods when they succeed, but isolated, wretched humans when a business fails. It's a story that ancient Greek poet Homer would recognize as his own.

CHAPTER 7.
CHURN CELEBRATED

The Entrepreneurial Myth distorts failure, skews success and promotes business churn.

SUCCESS IS EASY

The Entrepreneurial Myth depicts the entrepreneur as a special sage and top-tips guru. The sweat, blood and tears of real business is relegated to the small print; Business is easy! Follow these tips! You are encouraged to follow a handful of men; Richard Branson, Steve Jobs, Elon Musk, Jack Ma, perhaps a few more. You are urged to read his biography and follow his plan. And don't worry about failure. "I've been failing for as long as I can remember," says Branson. "If you aren't failing, you are not innovating enough," says Musk.[37] Can you hear the echo of ancient plots? Eureka, challenge and triumph; struggle, grow and sell.

This is the Myth at its most intoxicating because it blends two psychological phenomena. First, you are programmed to believe the quick fix tips. The truth bias[38] is the tendency to believe positive information from someone in authority whether it is true or not. Second, you are hard-wired to be impatient. It is psychologically uncomfortable to wait: instant gratification feels good. Which would you prefer to read: 'Four tips for building a million-dollar business' or 'How to build a million-dollar business in 14 years'? Quite! Oversimplified 'easy if you know how' top tips sit in stark contrast with the long slog of messy business. If business success really could be captured in top tips or quick fixes, entrepreneurial survival rates would not make such brutal reading. Now add the familiar shorthand of ancient stories and you are hooked.

Ironically, those promoting business risk and distorting failure, do so from a position of success and wealth. Davidow and Williams capture this neatly as they urge us all to Fail Brilliantly.[39] If Branson wasn't a success, you wouldn't hear his tale of failure. Success gives star entrepreneurs the platform, but hollows out their message. Those who are arguably as talented but didn't receive the break or the call – the real failures, if you like – remain invisible. What do they have to say about the ache of not quite making it? "Let's be honest, 'fail often: fail better' can be seen as the mantra of the privileged," say Davidow and Williams. "Those few who already know the taste of success in their fields – people not deterred by the results of their meandering experiments and associated risk factors." For those that don't make it onto the platform, failure is relentlessly personal.

FAILURE IS PERSONAL

The majority of entrepreneurial businesses fail yet, curiously, systematic study of this failure is muted. It remains an academic "weed patch rather than a well-tended garden"[40] with inconsistent theories and clashing ideas. Academics perpetuate The Entrepreneurial Myth too. Research tends to veer away from collective analysis of insolvency towards an entrepreneur's individual experience of trauma, stigma and learning. Swallowed shame and personalized grief are the focus; not the economics of cash flow, not the politics of international trade, not the psychology of customer demand. This must change.

Technically, statistically, most people fail and most businesses fail. "It is logistically impossible for seven billion people to rise to the top of the pile," deadpan Davidow and Williams.[41] Perfect sense, of course. But The Entrepreneurial Myth whispers: go on, have a shot, rise at five, tough it out. The Myth holds real business to an impossible standard by selling contextual failure as catastrophic failure.

As Davidow and Williams assert, not all failures are equal.[42] While first-degree failure is the unequivocal disaster of death or catastrophe, second-degree failure refers to the adventures of scientists, artists, engineers and entrepreneurs. This is the trial and error of discovery. Much of shared human endeavour balances here as the medical mistake creating a new drug or the disgraced adventurer discovering a new country on the way home. Third-degree failure is your personal quest for success and progress. This quest is defined by the inherited strivings and constructed standards shaping success and failure for you. This is the unique cross you bear.

Borrowing Davidow and Williams' analysis, see how The Entrepreneurial Myth trades the third-degree failure of personal entrepreneurial ambition for the jeopardy of national health, wealth and culture. The Entrepreneurial Myth raises the stakes. It spins a failed business as a shameful, public, first-degree disaster, not the personal third-degree disappointment it really is.

BUSINESS CHURN IS PROMOTED

Skewed attitudes to success and failure means business churn – the pace of businesses being created, folding into insolvency, new businesses being created again – is tolerated and promoted. Listen to entrepreneur turned Chairman of the Scottish Government's enterprise quango, Bob Keiller:[43] "with vast changes taking place in society, some businesses are under threat. Many in the retail sector, for example, have been in business for decades but can no longer make ends meet. We can't rely on existing companies to innovate. We need to keep replacing the stock of businesses with new businesses doing things differently. We need a continual flow of new businesses; we should encourage more start-ups to keep the enterprise funnel healthy. We need to recognize that most do not go on to be big businesses. Most tend to be sole traders or micro businesses and that's okay provided some grow. A healthy society encourages people to create and develop new ideas in the sheer knowledge that many won't go anywhere. It's a genetic process of mutation; only some of these mutations will become very successful and create new opportunities for people. If we stop this process, we'll lose out."

He continues: "The right idea might be to churn businesses quicker. Someone might start a business and it takes two years to realize that it will never fly. What if we can reach the same conclusion after just three months and move them on to something more likely to succeed? Isn't that better? Then they can add something to the economy, rather than wasting their time and support resources. In the world of innovation, we're taught to fail fast and fail cheaply. Why not apply that to business start-ups? If your first four businesses don't work but your fifth one does, how quickly can we get you on to your fifth? We need to quickly get you in front of customers to work out if they are willing to pay what you think. The customer is the ultimate arbiter of business success. We need to quickly put your plan it in front of investors to hear whether they would invest in you or not. We need to quickly get your team up the management ladder. Speed is more important than how well I can support you through your first four businesses. It's wasteful to take a long time to make these decisions and still conclude that this business is not going anywhere."

Pure economic perspectives like this say more is better; more ideas and more businesses, equals more success and more wealth. So, keep the funnel fed. However, this 'fifth time lucky' equation doesn't seem to account for the unquantifiable personal cost – the mental health challenge of failing and the trauma of losing a business. This equation doesn't include the significant transaction costs of business start-up and shut down in an imperfect market. It doesn't consider shared, systematic, macroeconomic causes for business failure – and the possibility of shared solutions.

But more of this in Chapter 14 with the opportunity to rethink enterprise policy and gently shift new business support towards scale-up sustainability. Arguably, only enterprise policy tolerates the almost certain probability of losing the millions invested.

For now, consider the distortions in how The Entrepreneurial Myth frames and fetishizes failure. Billion-dollar venture capitalist Khosla, for example, is one of many who pursue the peculiar global glamour of terrible odds: "I'm only interested in technologies that have a 90% chance of failure," he says. "But, if they do succeed, they would change the infrastructure of society in some radical way."[44] Why? There has to be a better way, with better odds.

CHAPTER 8.
ENTREPRENEUR ISOLATED

While distorting real business talent, success and failure, The Entrepreneurial Myth isolates and burdens business protagonists. A business creator intellectually understands the business journey will be difficult. Yet the seductive Myth – remember Aristotle's peripeteia – fuels the ego to believe in deserved recognition and inevitable fortunes just around the corner. Of course, it sometimes happens: there are glorious business stories and surprises. But oversimplifying real business quests and voyages and rags to riches journeys presents a comforting archetypal plot. The Myth can't prepare you for the grit and detail of real business.

An entrepreneur's life isn't lived in a dreamy soft focus. Your experience of time is not, as Newton argued, the uniform tick of 24 equal parts. Not every hour is equal or, to quote Cervantes, all times are not the same. Business protagonists experience time at different rates; from the sluggish wait for a client to pay to the rush of multitasking. It's notoriously hard to maintain perspective when your nose is pressed to the grindstone. The relentless detailed work demanded by a growing business is painful. When at the kitchen table in the small hours drafting a proposal to catch a customer or sitting in your car after a tough pitch, the entrepreneur knows, deep down, that guts are not enough. There is an unspoken and unseen need for sleep and support, coffee, coaching and community. Yet, the simplistic rags to riches stories whisk away a community of weather-beaten entrepreneurs who sat in the same place last year. And as economic individualism – the fuel of The Entrepreneurial Myth – has triumphed, people become increasingly more isolated and unhappier.[45]

You're no victim, though. Entrepreneurs build and collude and play with the Myth themselves.

I WANNA BE ADORED

Believing is seeing.[46] Metaphor helps entrepreneurs make decisions,[47] solve problems[48] and spot opportunities.[49] Word choice thus becomes a key managerial tool.[50] Much of the modern business environment is built on metaphor. Consider Boston Consulting Group's growth share matrix with dogs and cash cows, Porter's value chain, Moore's predators, prey and ecosystem, Kotler and Singh's battle strategy or Nalebuff's games. All reek of myth; we think, study and work in metaphor.

The Entrepreneurial Myth is irresistible to those at its heart. It's a dilemma. You like people thinking you are special. The Myth sometimes feels good. You use it as shorthand for who you are. Archetypal plots are so ingrained in the human psyche, you follow the script in real life. It becomes a huge risk to ego and reputation, perhaps even to your business in smaller communities, to step outside the fairy tale. A business' employees and sales rest on your confidence. A business' success rests on your special status. It can be lonely in this double bind: consider the courage required to prove the Myth wrong by asking another entrepreneur if they feel the same. The Myth's price is paid with mental health and well-being.

The business protagonist is isolated by The Entrepreneurial Myth but also by the shape of the business built. Relationships built through water-cooler gossip mitigate stress and boost mental well-being. But entrepreneurs, with just a handful of employees and perhaps no workplace superiors, lack the social support found in larger corporate structures. Instead, entrepreneurs plug a psychological gap with encouraging customer or employee feedback and by deliberately creating family-like bonds with the first employees. Business becomes utterly personal. A cross-sectional study found entrepreneurs feel uniquely responsible for the people they employ to the detriment of their mental well-being.[51] This segregation takes place in The Lonely City[52] where a peculiar tension forms between the external noise, buzz and clash of your start-up office, and the "uneasy combination of separation and exposure" demanded by an entrepreneurial role.

Here is a perfect psychological storm: the dissonance between 'easy business' and your daily reality, the queasy knowledge that your entrepreneurial gut isn't quite enough, plus skewed failure, loneliness and a brooding employee burden.

There are entrepreneurial networks designed to combat isolation but many unwittingly fuel the Myth with halls of fame, top tips and award ceremonies to reward archetypal stories and rags to riches triumphs. Connecting one entrepreneur to another is not enough. The conversation held when they meet needs to be different. Without releasing entrepreneurs from the Myth's overarching narrative – and creating a new one – organized entrepreneurial networks may struggle to serve real businesses.

CHAPTER 9.
MENTAL HEALTH COMPROMISED

You have heard how The Entrepreneurial Myth excludes talent, demonizes weakness, isolates entrepreneurs, and skews attitudes to success and failure. For all these reasons, the Myth jeopardises entrepreneurial mental health. High-profile suicides[53] of entrepreneurs spark justified soul-searching. Why did someone so special feel so wretched?

It is impossible to understand entrepreneurial mental health struggles and suicide without first hearing the relentless, hectoring voices of The Entrepreneurial Myth. The voices weave through every form of modern media, through business schools, politics and policy: believe in tough trials, but easy success. Follow the top ten tips, follow your gut, follow Steve. Create jobs, make money, spark joy. These incessant voices bounce feebly off emerging statistics regarding entrepreneurial mental health.

Listen to this. One of the first studies[54] to link higher rates of mental health issues with entrepreneurship found 49% of the sampled entrepreneurs in the US reported mental health conditions. Depression was number one with 30% of sampled entrepreneurs experiencing the condition compared with 15% of the study's non-entrepreneurial control group. A significant proportion, 29%, experienced Attention Deficit Hyperactivity Disorder, with 27% experiencing anxiety problems.[55]

Is this a surprise? Anecdotally, high levels of anxiety and feelings of being overwhelmed seem ubiquitous for entrepreneurs. 'Tell all' stories – like Rand Fishkin's *Lost and Founder: A Painfully Honest Field Guide to the Startup World*[56] – help fill in the gaps between the statistics. While UK statistics don't break down mental health conditions or suicide rates by occupation, there is growing anecdotal evidence from London's silicon roundabout. Consider the podcast, *Killing It*, created by tech journalist and psychologist Aleks Krotoski. Six raw episodes gently start to unpick damaging tech community habits with a radical openness. Everything definitely isn't awesome all the time. Instead, there are stories of burnout, depression and loneliness; mania, insomnia and stress. Similarly, Mark Leruste's podcast series' *The Unconventionalists* and *The Doubt* include discussion about the shadow of entrepreneurial success.

Ironically, other blogs and articles[57] on entrepreneurial mental health – designed to be kind, candid, revolutionary even – unwittingly make the problem worse. "Depression happens to extraordinary people," one writer claims, unknowingly advancing Entrepreneurial Mythology. "It's something you can work through if you treat it like a hurdle instead of a defect." Simultaneously dismissive and competitive, this sentence turns depression into a performance issue. The illustrative case studies in these profiles of mental health struggles always end well. Listen to this dangerous voyage and return plot: **sales plummeted 75%. He had exhausted his assets and laid-off his team. He locked himself in his room with his guitar**. But, then, guess what?! He kept working, scored his biggest ever contract and sales are up 5,000%. **He's more resilient now, tempered by tough times**. Meet another man, hours from losing his home, saved by a 300-page contract and a strategic investor. "I'm going to remember this," he says dryly. "It's the farthest I'm willing to go."

There can sometimes be a psychological kickback from entrepreneurial struggle. Colin Brett – a psychotherapist who has coached thousands of entrepreneurs and whose interview is featured in Chapter 19 – calls this the heroism of hard work. There is an undeniable social buzz of sympathy surrounding ferocious hard work. It is at its loudest in workplaces that competitively value hours served, rather than productivity. You can get addicted to sharing martyred stories of workplace sacrifice, Brett explains. Success stories don't hold the same social or psychological power.

Commentators chirp solutions for the burnt-out entrepreneur: take some cardiovascular exercise, avoid sugar, meditate for 20 minutes a day, have a dinner with your spouse once a month. **Don't worry, aiming high can make you feel like shit sometimes**. Remember **creative moments often follow a depressive episode**.

But these well-meaning platitudes miss the point. The Entrepreneurial Myth is a collective schema, a shared mental map, that insists the collective burden of enterprise is carried by a special individual. Whatever the cost. The weight of these community expectations urges an entrepreneur to keep going, clear the mental health hurdle, then write a blog about the business lesson learned.

Open corporate cultures and leaders' tears must only be part of a broader, kinder, structural solution. The collective burden of enterprise must be removed from entrepreneurs' shoulders alone and shared by the politicians, colleagues and customers that benefit. It's not good enough to shout **stay strong hustlers**, while promoting burnout seminars.

ALL BY MYSELF

At its heart, The Entrepreneurial Myth rests on an outdated assumption that an entrepreneur is defined by distinctive characteristics such as autonomy, focus and creativity. Academic William Gartner led the charge away from trait-theory with his classic article *'Who Is an Entrepreneur?' Is the Wrong Question*.[58] The overwhelming number of contradictory qualities that supposedly define an entrepreneur "portrays someone larger than life ... a sort of generic 'everyman'". Research should focus on what an entrepreneur does, not who they are. The academic gaze then shifted to the outcomes of entrepreneurial behaviour, such as the impact of risk propensity or of entrepreneurial intuition. The rest have not caught up. And, crucially, the agency and responsibility for the business remains anchored in the individual entrepreneur.

Biographers are particularly susceptible to burying greatness in an individual's guts and psyche. Life stories point to the special imbalances that drive the revered on. Consider the numerous profiles and biographies of Steve Jobs that linger on his cold charm as "a chosen one, an enlightened one."[59] Hear the rich biographical mythology in Jack Ma's *Eureka!* moment: "the idea of the internet had been circling round like an eagle in his mind ever since he had discussed it with Bill. Now he could see its shining feathers and eager eyes. He could hear it saying to him: 'Come on, Jack Ma, I will carry you up into the sky, to soar over the oceans and the earth.'"[60] Witness how Elon Musk's biographer[61] unwittingly shapes his subject's life story to fit the Myth. Musk is called to greatness and sees "man's fate in the Universe as a personal obligation."[62] He's a "Silicon Valley deity" trying to "soothe a type of existential depression that seems to gnaw at his every fiber."[63] There are epic challenges to overcome in a "saga packed full of ambition, dodgy manoeuvring, brutal politics."[64] But rest assured, reader, Musk will triumph in the end. "Squint ever so slightly," sighs the biographer, "and it looks like Musk could be using his skills to pave the way toward an age of astonishing machines and science fiction dreams made manifest."[65]

It's convenient to locate the success of an organization in an individual. It serves the businesses, communities and economies that surround the business protagonist. Just as news is shorthand for a chaotic reality stuffed with numerous potential stories. Just as policy is shorthand for an infinite political will to change society one way or another. So, an entrepreneur's body, mind and behaviour become shorthand for messy business. There is a physical body to contain the hopes and aspirations and economic necessities of enterprise. The news, enterprise policy, even the entrepreneur himself, are maps and tools used to handle complexity. Academic reasoning has evolved away from entrepreneurial trait theory but the media still favours its simplicity and brevity. And this means that when a business protagonist's mental health falters, The Entrepreneurial Myth makes it personal.

An entrepreneur's nature makes him vulnerable to the dark side of obsession,[66] says a popular business blog. Entrepreneurs pile pressure on themselves, sighs another. Entrepreneurs harbour secret demons, claims a leading business magazine. Potentially deadly struggles with mental health shrink to an internalized challenge hidden from a wildly enthusiastic crowd. And how perilous it is to conceptualize depression as a monster to conquer.

YOU MAKE ME SICK

The World Health Organization defines mental health as a state of well-being in which every individual can realize his or her potential, can cope with the normal stresses of life and work productively to contribute to his or her community. This rightly places entrepreneurial mental health in a broad, expansive landscape. Mental health is a continuum of blended psychiatric, psychological and emotional states, which goes well beyond the tight medicalized definitions found in the International Classification of Diseases.[67]

In this context, a thorough review of research[68] on entrepreneurial mental health dips into business schools, industry forums and conference circuits. It draws on economics, organizational psychology, occupational health, management and social sciences. Remember, entrepreneurs are not a homogenous gang. There is a difference between those who are entrepreneurs through necessity – through job loss or cultural context, perhaps – and those who chase a specific opportunity. An economic push into entrepreneurship versus the pull of an opportunistic vision influences business leaders' well-being. But overall, entrepreneurial work is more uncertain, more complex, more stressful and more pressured than corporate work. Entrepreneurs typically earn less than employees. "Why would anyone voluntarily accept the longer work hours, fewer weekends and holidays, more responsibility, chronic uncertainty, greater personal risk and struggle, and greater investment of emotional and physical resources required to be an entrepreneur instead of the security and long-term rewards of having a career?" asks Freeman.[69] "By conventional standards, choosing to be an entrepreneur is an exercise in bad judgement."

Some entrepreneurs interpret long working hours and a stressful environment as a mark of business success. Thus, business protagonists define their organization as entrepreneurial *because* it is intense, pressurized and stressful. Stress is considered an essential characteristic of an entrepreneurial business. And if the pace and pressure eases, the business somehow feels less entrepreneurial. Similarly, research reveals mental well-being is perceived as an indicator of entrepreneurial success. Hear the bravado: killing it, smashing it, crushing it!

Something curious is happening here. An entrepreneurial business is a stressful business, thus an entrepreneur is a stressed person. But a successful entrepreneur is someone who doesn't appear stressed. The entrepreneur is in a perfect double bind. And the pinch can be deadly; feelings of being trapped have been proven to be a more significant predictor of suicide than depression. Focus narrows, so suicide mistakenly seems the only escape from the relentless Herculean trials of business in a tough economy.

Just as a business is defined as entrepreneurial because it is pressurized, so an entrepreneur takes his or her identity from the pressure experienced. Research confirms what an entrepreneur sees in a bad set of figures; financial problems in an entrepreneurial business hurt beyond their material impact. Poor performance, job loss, public perception of business success and the cold fear of failure threatens entrepreneurs' self-image and identity in a way that leaves regular employees unmoved. Business identity and personal identity are entwined. With work at heart, job satisfaction is knotted with life satisfaction. This tangle is then glossed with the public expectation that a successful entrepreneur is forever happy, healthy and wealthy.

Something always gives. The trade-off for satisfying work is lower wages or less leisure time. The trade-off for autonomy is isolation, perhaps obsession. The trade-off for being perceived a success, essential to your identity as an entrepreneur, is transparency. Research implies there may be a self-justification process in entrepreneurs to avoid cognitive dissonance, or the mental discomfort of holding two contradictory beliefs or values. This is the psychological trade-off. It says: I cannot exchange working in my business for less money and less family time, if I am not happy. The personal and financial cost is only justified with reports of vigorous job satisfaction and a glamourous life – the ultimate entrepreneurial benefits. Consequently, self-reported statistics of entrepreneurial satisfaction should be approached with caution. There is too much to lose. The Entrepreneurial Myth has created an entrepreneurial mask with severe consequences for the health and well-being of business protagonists.

SILVER LINING

The Entrepreneurial Myth looks on the bright side. Imbalances in mental health could be used to great effect, it is claimed in a respected journal. Attention Deficit Hyperactivity Disorder offers the business community risk takers with restless drive. Narcissism supplies powerful, persuasive personalities. Autism Spectrum Disorder offers the business community hyper-focused detail and discovery. There is evidence that entrepreneurs experience higher rates of Bipolar Disorder characterized by leaps in imagination and impulsive energy.[70] Research[71] suggests that there are functional aspects to mental health challenges that support entrepreneurial behaviour. Persistent negative emotion fuels some entrepreneurs with enhanced short-term focus. It's not just entrepreneurial to avoid mental health problems; entrepreneurial behaviour is perversely characterized by mental health problems.

Theorists hypothesize[72] that plotting entrepreneurial benefits against the severity of mental health problems forms an inverse curve. The impulsivity component of Attention Deficit Hyperactivity Disorder, for example, may be related to opportunity development and entrepreneurial orientation. But if the condition sharpens, entrepreneurial orientation is subdued. There is also an inverse U-shaped relationship between the intensity of meaningful entrepreneurial work and founder mental well-being. Intense, demanding work – the classic start-up cocktail – promotes short-term mental well-being. But that positive effect can tip into all-consuming damage as the pressure ramps up. The body adapts and protects itself for the fight to come but unrelenting exposure to stress factors causes allostatic load. The wear and tear effects of sustained exposure to chronic stress predisposes entrepreneurs to mental health problems over the longer term.

Perhaps other disorders and symptoms can be functional for certain types of entrepreneurial action, muses a researcher. This would change your perception of mental disorder, she concludes. This book proposes the opposite: the relationship between entrepreneurs and mental health challenges should change your perception of entrepreneurship. A world view that values or causes or promotes mental health problems for economic benefit must be examined and challenged.

"If you are manic, you think you're Jesus," says one author. "If you're hypomanic, you think you're God's gift to technology investing. We're talking about different levels of grandiosity but the same symptoms."[73] Hypomania may be responsible for some entrepreneurs' strengths as well as their flaws, he concludes.

Stop. Take a step back. Let's not look on the bright side of mental illness for economic gain. The dark heart of The Entrepreneurial Myth keeps entrepreneurs sick as the economy and community that surrounds them benefit from the empires they build.

CHAPTER 10.
LOST THE PLOT

Remember, plots are mental maps located in specific culture. Booker's seven plots have deep roots in the Graeco-Roman tradition, so are unavoidably culturally skewed. If you examine Chinese mythology, it still offers dragons to defeat, tragedies and epic quests to carry the moral values of Taoism, Confucianism and Buddhism. But public good and the brave pursuit of a better life are unequivocally valued more than individual heroics.

During the Chinese Cultural Revolution, many myths that symbolized old customs and superstitions were destroyed; others were rewritten to deliver a political point. Mao Zedong, for example, rewrote the myth of Gong Gong fighting against Zhuan to be the Supreme Divinity as a way of praising rebellion against the established order. Since the 1980s, there has been a resurgence of popular myth in China. Folk traditions have been turned into cultural resources to build local identity, engage tourists and develop the economy.[74]

A brilliant example of repurposing traditional myth for modern ambitions is *The Legend of Nezha*, a popular animated series produced by Central China Television in 2003.[75] The series tells of a child, Nezha, who is trained to battle evil through a series of struggles, just like Booker's quest plot. But the twist comes in a new moral message, not present in the original myth, but now applied to the modern cartoon. In the ancient story, Kuafu pursues the sun and no-one is sure why. Perhaps ego; perhaps doomed competitiveness. Either way, before he reaches the sun, he dies of thirst. In the TV series, Kuafu is recast to represent justice and self-devotion. Instead of the story ending with Kuafu's death, he changes into a forest to guide people toward the sun. Nihilistic bleakness is replaced with a tale of human courage, ambition and persistence in the face of impossible odds. Retold in numerous Chinese poems, novels and films, the legend has evolved to fit The Entrepreneurial Myth. It says: don't give up, your ambition will be rewarded.

Indian mythology similarly enjoys a large cast of deities and demigods who battle in a power struggle for celestial worlds. Heroes pit honesty against deceit, compassion against cruelty, and fairness against greed. Ancient stories still weave through modern culture in India, informing modern art, film and festivals. Rich fables, such as *The Mouse Merchant*[76] unintentionally inform and promote The Entrepreneurial Myth. *The Mouse Merchant* is a fatherless boy who sells a dead mouse to a cat-owner for corn; exchanges the corn for wood; and eventually sells the wood to the townspeople who scorned him. All to illustrate business-savvy ideals of fortitude and perseverance.

The Entrepreneurial Myth spans radically different countries, tens of thousands of miles apart, with roots in the fundamentally different world views of Christianity,

Confucianism and Buddhism. Yet beyond Booker's analysis, Chinese and Indian myth reveal similar plots that shape the countries' psyche; a call to greatness, a path strewn with challenges, but rich rewards await. The Entrepreneurial Myth bridges the radically different economies of the UK, US, China and India. While UK and US economies have established, institutionalized entrepreneurial cultures, Chinese and Indian economic models are evolving. Does the hyperbole of the Myth in the UK and US, with the consequences and inefficiencies of entrepreneurship in these markets, serve as a helpful warning to entrepreneurial colleagues in China and India? Could these countries avoid the Myth's extremes and move straight to a more reflective, effective entrepreneurship?

Just as the Myth spans oceans and geographies, so it spans time and centuries. Plots are mental maps located in specific time. Just as newspaper stories have changed over 30 years, so too have the seven universal plots. New Romanticism changed Europe's psychological 'centre of gravity'[77] in the 18th century, influencing music, painting and the arts. This intellectual movement was characterized by individualism. Intuition was valued above all else. The cultural shift detached stories from their underlying archetypal purpose. Plots no longer depict an internal transformation, instead the cinematic focus is on changing outward circumstances alone. This, Booker asserts, ends in sickly sentimentalism, or obsession with sex and violence. Plots revolve hopelessly around tinsel and glitter, but nothing really happens at all.

This dislocation of the map from its meaning may explain the futility of The Entrepreneurial Myth. It suggests a reason for the increasing ferocity of stories covering entrepreneurial failures. It may explain the dislocation between the Myth and the experience of women, people working within transitional economies or anyone who isn't WASP-ish white.

The Myth's stories can't satisfy because the focus is on the external business, not the inward development of the business protagonist. The entrepreneur believes the Myth: "this business quest will be the making of me." But internal transformation isn't possible while the focus is on the product or the office or the external business. The mistake is to confuse external symbols for inward transformation. The Entrepreneurial Myth furiously peddles a cinematic illusion: *Eureka!* Funding. Growth. Success. Sales. The Myth is mawkish and sentimental. Reach for the stars! Leap before you look! Follow these top ten tips to insane success!

But it is not easy. Hear the frustration of those leading the 90% of businesses that fail or the business owners fighting a disproportionate share of mental health issues. Without looking after the business protagonist, business creation is futile. If we remove the potential for inward transformation from entrepreneurial stories, it is no wonder the real business experience sometimes feels so empty.

To make room for the inner transformation promised by great business, you must change the exclusion and isolation, distortion and damage at the heart of the global Entrepreneurial Myth.

HURRY UP!

And do it now. Initial calculations show that if the Myth was tempered and business success rates improved by 10%, it could be worth £19.6 billion to the UK economy and $850 billion to the US economy. Now imagine the prize in China, in India. Add the priceless human benefit of preserving entrepreneurial mental health and well-being. While the Myth is not new, there has never been a better time to challenge it and strip it of its power, to build something better in its place.

IN BRIEF:
PSYCHOLOGY

- The Entrepreneurial Myth excludes talent from real business by insisting that an entrepreneur is 'not one of us' and this creates a barrier to people who don't fit the entrepreneurial stereotype of a white, Western man. The Myth is unapologetically male.
- The Entrepreneurial Myth demonizes weakness and isolates entrepreneurs with the lie that the answer to business success is buried in their guts.
- The Entrepreneurial Myth distorts attitudes to success and failure. The Myth insists business is easy, when it's not. The Myth makes failure personal and catastrophic, when a proportion of business failure is systematic and simply disappointing. This possibly heightens business churn.
- For all these reasons, The Entrepreneurial Myth potentially jeopardizes entrepreneurial mental health and well-being. Initial research reveals entrepreneurs report significantly higher proportion of mental health challenges. With no inference

regarding causation or correlation, it remains important to reconsider stories of entrepreneurial mania, depression, loneliness and burnout. Does entrepreneurship trade health for wealth?

- This is potentially a global problem as economies and attitudes to entrepreneurship converge.

The analysis rests on three pillars. The first pillar was the ancient history of storytelling, myth and metaphor to understand why we deify entrepreneurs. The second pillar was social psychology, to analyse the personal impact of The Entrepreneurial Myth on individual business creators. Now we turn to the third pillar of economics, to explore the costly economic exchange society makes for the inefficiencies of The Entrepreneurial Myth.

PART 3.

ECONOMICS.
CREATIVE
DISTRACTION

CHAPTER 11.
CENTRE STAGE

The entrepreneur doesn't stand in an empty arena; economic history and political staging drive The Entrepreneurial Myth. Standing in the wings are two grandfathers of modern economics, Adam Smith and Joseph Schumpeter. Both viewed the entrepreneur as the source of economic growth. Both believed the merchant, baker and entrepreneur should be free to do what they do best without interference and urged government restraint so business strategy remained unfettered by political will. Both unwittingly kindled The Entrepreneurial Myth.

In the 18th century, Adam Smith revealed the 'invisible hand' of market forces – the natural balance of supply and demand when untouched by meddling institutions – and pushed the merchant to the heart of what would become laissez-faire economic policy. "It is not from the benevolence of the butcher, the brewer or the baker that we expect our dinner," he famously claimed. "But from their regard to their own interest."[78] The entrepreneur is an active agent of capitalism, helpfully serving us all through his self-interest.

Smith's ideas, now archetypal economic theories, were the cornerstone of the classical school of economics.

Fast forward to the 20th century and a more argumentative figure, Joseph Schumpeter, shaped neoclassical economics. The entrepreneur remained centre stage: "without innovation, no entrepreneurs; without entrepreneurial achievement, no capitalist returns and no capitalist propulsion."[79] Leadership, not ownership, is what matters. The energetic, internal drive of the entrepreneur generates waves of 'creative destruction'. This is the relentless surge of technological innovation that reinvents markets and increases living standards by declaring yesterday's products and services obsolete. In a healthy Schumpeterian economy, all profit is temporary, bankruptcy is inevitable and monopolies fail as the next big thing breaks. Like Aristotle's wheel, fragile fortunes rise and fall around the entrepreneur.

DO SOMETHING!

These enduring ideas influence economics, business and news today. Adam Smith stares from the Bank of England's £20 note; Schumpeter still has a column in *The Economist* magazine! Like Statler and Waldorf, their commentary – part inherited, part imagined – informs enterprise policy. Layers of party-political ideology have been superimposed over these economic principles. Winston Churchill put it best: "Some people regard private enterprise as a predatory tiger to be shot," he said. "Others look on it as a cow they can milk. Not enough people see it as a healthy horse, pulling a sturdy wagon." Those on the left see private business as a predator; moderates want the milk;

others see enterprise as an essential component of the capitalist system. Compare David Cameron's "party of start-ups, go-getters and risk-takers"[80] with Jeremy Corbyn's pledge[81], seven years later, to end the "magical thinking of the free market that has led to a minority becoming extremely rich at the expense of everybody else."

Whatever the political hue, most agree entrepreneurship has a key role to play in facilitating wealth and growth. Big business may be seen as fair game on the left of the political spectrum, but small and medium sized business enjoys broad cross-party support. The debate rages over retained versus redistributed entrepreneurial wealth. Yet, whatever product is made, or tax paid, the entrepreneur remains a convenient god of enterprise and industry. Politicians still claim the entrepreneur facilitates prosperity and social freedom; and by paying a bit more tax or paying their workers better, can help the government upgrade creaking infrastructure.[82]

Rhetoric is converted to policy, but short-termism rules. In a four- or five-year election cycle or presidential term, an enterprise initiative barely has time to be printed and implemented before the start-up it is designed to serve, fails. Consider the churn of entrepreneurial schemes launched, deleted, renamed, duplicated and repeated by successive governments[83] keen to 'do something'. Funds are distributed; then cancelled. UK Enterprise Zones, for example, were abandoned after a 15-year run under Thatcher and Major governments, but repurposed and relaunched under David Cameron in 2011.

Party lines drive these decisions, but at a considerable transaction cost. Business momentum is inevitably lost when schemes are repeatedly swapped. The churn of hubs, funds and initiatives becomes impossible to navigate in the daily hustle of real business. Consequently, The Entrepreneurial Myth is perpetuated by short-term policy. And the policy doesn't work. Policy does not facilitate Schumpeter's creative destruction, instead it is a creative *distraction*. Consider these enterprise initiatives in the UK and the US from the past 50 years.

Whether 'special friends' or now more cautious allies, the UK and US have shared similar attitudes and approaches to entrepreneurship for decades. If UK and US enterprise policy is considered side by side, it is possible to trace the role of the entrepreneur simultaneously morphing from job creator, recession rescuer, equality warrior, to finally become the nation's inspiration. Broadly the same policy path has been chosen by two Western democracies over a 40-year period. This hints at a movement bigger than the fluctuations of party-political leanings; a global philosophical swell of entrepreneurial myth-making, perhaps? Since Smith and Schumpeter first ushered the entrepreneur on stage, the role has grown from the narrow economic purity of job creation, to a national source of moral inspiration. Rhetoric has escalated as the collective responsibility for enterprise and wealth creation has been placed on entrepreneurs' shoulders. Listen to this ...

CHAPTER 12.
SPECIAL FRIENDS

THE UNITED KINGDOM AND THE UNITED STATES: 1979 TO THE PRESENT DAY
GIVE ME A JOB (1979 TO 1989)

In the UK, 1970s economic policy focused on increasing the quantity of businesses, with associated job creation targets.[84] Reaction to economic difficulty was uncompromising and offered little support for entrepreneurs. Then, Margaret Thatcher[85] was elected. Thatcher launched her administration with a deliberate intent to "change Britain from a dependent to a self-reliant society; from a give-it-to-me, to a do-it-yourself nation; a get-up-and-go, instead of a sit-back-and-wait-for-it Britain."[86] She was possibly the first to say it: "This means creating a new culture – an enterprise culture – which accords a new status to the entrepreneur and offers him the rewards to match; which breeds a new generation of men and women who create jobs for others instead of waiting for others to create jobs for them."[87]

Not all agreed that Thatcher promoted entrepreneurship from an ideological position;[88] perhaps enterprise culture simply offered a deeply pragmatic solution to endemic unemployment. Either way, Thatcher was dubbed the 'Entrepreneur's Prime Minister' for her emphasis on freeing small businesses to play a starring role in the UK's new prosperity. The Thatcher government dramatically increased the number of enterprise policy initiatives;[89] the Enterprise Allowance Scheme supported entrepreneurs for up to a year as their businesses grew; the top rate of income tax was halved to reward high earners; and Enterprise Zones clustered the services and support demanded by small businesses. In the vivid words of Ruth Lea, then head of policy at the Institute of Directors, Thatcher "took the burdens off business and let animal spirits take over."[90] Just like Hercules' lion.

The results were dramatic. In June 1989, business start-ups, net of liquidations, sprung into life at the furious pace of 1,300 a week.[91] The UK enterprise population grew from 2.4 million businesses in 1980, to 3.6 million in 1989.[92] The 'hands off', 'entrepreneur knows best', policy philosophy exposed vulnerabilities in the manufacturing sector.

Churn was an issue; one in six entrepreneurial businesses assisted by the Enterprise Allowance Scheme didn't make it to their first anniversary. But many of the scheme's beneficiaries were one-person operations which successfully forged new cultural and arts-related businesses. This broadened the UK's services sector and produced entrepreneurial stars like Creation Records founder Alan McGee, and *Viz* comic founder Chris Donald.

The emphasis for wealth creation shifted from industrial competitiveness to celebrating the entrepreneur and their talents. Archetypal rags-to-riches stories blended with the political rhetoric precisely when the economy of the late 1970s – with its debt, unemployment and recession – desperately craved an economic saviour. The modern Entrepreneurial Myth was finally born.

Prime Minister Thatcher and US President Ronald Reagan[93] were political soulmates.[94] Both were influenced by the job creation philosophies of David Birch[95] whose research demonstrated how small firms with fewer than 20 employees created 66% of net new jobs across all sectors of the US economy, while 81% of net new jobs were created by firms with fewer than 100 employees. Jobs were the prize; the more, the better. So, echoing Thatcher's Enterprise Culture, Americans were promised a 'Reagan Revolution'. It was focused on reducing government taxes and regulation to boost post-recession economic growth with innovation and entrepreneurship.

Familiar with the film scripts of adventure quests, the former movie actor effortlessly sold The Entrepreneurial Myth; "too often, entrepreneurs are forgotten heroes," said Reagan.[96] "We rarely hear about them. But look into the heart of America, and you'll see them. They're the brave people everywhere who produce our goods, feed a hungry world, and keep our homes and families warm while they invest in the future to build a better America."

Statute and policy followed; four federal laws[97] were passed to fund and support small businesses. This shifted the US from a managed economy with regulation suited to large enterprises, towards a free(r) market economy focused on fuelling entrepreneurial start-ups. The start-up rates increased through the 1980s and 1990s – yet most failed within the first five years. Nevertheless, with film star flair, Reagan's rhetoric continued:[98] "Why not set out with your friends on the path of adventure and try to start up your own business? Follow in the footsteps of those two college students who launched one of America's great computer firms from the garage behind their house. You, too, can help us unlock the doors to a golden future. You, too, can become leaders in this great new era of progress – the age of the entrepreneur." Here's what happened next ...

RESCUE FROM RECESSION (1989 TO 1997)

US President George H.W. Bush[99] presided over six quarters of economic decline. He emphasized the private sector, rather than government, as the engine of economic growth to power out of the doldrums. Ushering in the Small Business Credit and Business Opportunity Enhancement Act 1992, Bush declared that "this bill ensures that capital, the lifeblood of our economy, is available to help small firms start up." His Agenda for American Renewal focused on free trade and global economic competition, incentives for business and 'rightsizing' government. But Bush's presidential term was dominated by foreign policy, the end of the Cold War and the fall of the Berlin Wall. Despite the prospect of $20 billion in tax breaks for small business, Bush lost the 1992 presidential election to a fresh-faced Bill Clinton.

US President Clinton[100] backed $77 billion in loans to small business under the US Small Business Administration (SBA), a government agency designed to support entrepreneurs and strengthen the nation's economy. The SBA's Small Business Investment Company Programme doubled venture capital investments and a New Markets Initiative ploughed $15 billion of new investment into urban and rural areas. Legislation[101] was introduced to provide an estimated $20 billion in tax relief to small businesses and improve health insurance cover for the self-employed. Clinton sought the power behind the "engine of our entrepreneurship" by attempting to streamline government procurement with further legislation, with mixed results.

The SBA's focus on the 'hard' support of finance, access to government procurement and contracts advice, seemed to deliver value for money. Established in 1953, the SBA is a rare example of long-term thinking; its 60-year record of offering a stable and coherent suite of enterprise policies has borne fruit. US enterprise support was around $100 per capita less than UK expenditure – potentially because of the complexity of the UK's enterprise support schemes – so may represent a more effective funding model for entrepreneurs.[102]

In the UK, it wasn't until the 1990s that the policy imperative shifted to improving the productivity and quality of businesses, by developing the entrepreneurial skills and abilities of young people.[103] The Major government's[104] flagship policy, Business Link, was designed to streamline small business support with a network of personal business advisors; yet enterprise policy initiatives almost doubled between 1989 and 1996.[105] It proved incredibly difficult to pick the high growth potential businesses versus those whose owner-managers favoured business contraction or exit in the long-term.[106]

MAKE THIS WORLD A BETTER PLACE (1997 TO 2009)

The UK's Blair government[107] kept Business Link but developed additional policy to include potential entrepreneurs from traditionally under-represented groups. In the late 1990s to the late 2000s, principal policy objectives balanced national productivity and social inclusion. Blair urged entrepreneurs to become the front-line troops of Britain's new economy.[108] For the first time, entrepreneurship was gifted the power to solve societal challenges. The shift to encouraging, incentivizing and rewarding people to start-up businesses crowned the entrepreneur as economic saviour: "There is a new economic role for Government. We don't believe in laissez-faire. But the role is not picking winners, heavy-handed intervention, old-style corporatism, but: education, skills, technology, small business entrepreneurship."[109]

Yet enterprise initiatives, like The Small Business Service, were savaged by reports[110] that over 80% of small and medium sized businesses felt there had been no improvement in access to finance, and over 90% believed there had been no improvement in regulation and policy. In 2005, over 267[111] government enterprise support programmes greeted potential entrepreneurs. Where would you begin?

Stateside, President George W. Bush[112] trimmed capital gains taxes and streamlined tax reporting requirements for small business. Again, small business loans from the SBA were increased. A pro-growth stimulus package included cash-back tax rebates to encourage spending and 13 new free trade agreements.

A new UK government assumed power in 2007; Prime Minister Gordon Brown[113] immediately declared his intention to create a 'government of all the talents'. He offered ministerial jobs to non-politicians who were promptly nicknamed 'goats' by Westminster insiders; former secretary general of the Confederation of British Industry Digby Jones became minister for UK trade and investment; former City fund manager Paul Myners joined the Treasury, businessman Paul Drayson became Minister of State for Science and Innovation; Alan Sugar became Brown's politically neutral Enterprise Champion. Entrepreneurial businessmen became government insiders with an uncomfortable seat at the top table.

It was an uneasy relationship; goats are determined creatures and prone to locking horns when they know they're right. Public gaffs accentuated an uncomfortable alliance; civil servants were attacked[114] and most goats lasted no more than 18 months. In 2009, an influential paper[115] was published stating that, despite numerous government initiatives, there had been no improvement in rates of entrepreneurship and enterprise development since 1997.

During this period, Brown's premiership was interrupted, perhaps even prolonged, by one of the biggest financial shocks in history. A crisis in the US subprime mortgage market resulted in the collapse of investment bank Lehman Brothers on 15 September 2008. Brown led well in the midst of the crisis; cynicism about his leadership was temporarily suspended. He put entrepreneurship at the heart of post-recession recovery with a renewed commitment to "do everything we can to support and unleash the entrepreneurial, innovative and dynamic talents we know we have in Britain."[116]

The shock of the 2008 financial crisis soured trust in the financial services sector. Mysterious financial tricks like 'credit default swaps' were blamed for destroying the banks. So political voices cajoled the entrepreneur back to the good old days of manufacturing tangible products. The thin years following the Great Recession of the late noughties demanded the certainty of making things.

NATION'S INSPIRATION (2009 TO 2016)

US President Barack Obama[117] introduced the Recovery Act and Small Business Jobs Act to support over $93 billion in lending to more than 166,000 small businesses. More credit was available, complemented by 18 new tax cuts for small business, including credits for hiring unemployed workers and veterans. There were renewed efforts to award federal government contracts to small business owners; in the fiscal year 2015, more than a quarter of eligible contracts were awarded to entrepreneurs. An interesting regional perspective was deployed; $50 million was allocated to the Economic Development Administration to create regional innovation clusters designed to leverage regional competitive strengths. The Start-up America programme was launched to educate, mentor, fund and free up small firms. And as Prime Minister Gordon Brown welcomed his goats into the heart of government, Obama elevated the SBA to his cabinet. Similarly, this was largely interpreted as a symbolic gesture to highlight the ideological importance of small business in economic recovery. Obama's rhetoric favoured manufacturing over the services sector, especially if it included technology.

The UK's Cameron-Clegg coalition[118] also longed for "a Britain carried aloft by the march of the makers".[119] The coalition government published an enterprise policy paper outlining priorities between 2010 and 2015. Cameron infamously called for an 'enterprise-led recovery': "The recovery we need is a private sector-led recovery, a recovery with 'Made in Britain' stamped all over it. We need to see a country where new businesses are starting up on every street, in every town; where entrepreneurs are everywhere."[120]

Responding to Cameron's call, inspired by Start-up America, British entrepreneurs launched Start-up Britain, an organization designed to champion Britain's 270,000 annual start-up businesses. The associated Start-up Loans scheme distributed more than £300 million of loans to more than 46,000 start-ups. Government statistics report the number of entrepreneurial businesses subsequently jumped to 5.5 million and most of these businesses were either sole proprietorships or those employing more than ten people. Despite being 'by entrepreneurs, for entrepreneurs', success in delivering an increase in the number of female entrepreneurs was more muted.

Short-termism and enterprise indecision persisted. Enterprise Zones were resurrected, Regional Development Agencies were born and scrapped, Local Enterprise Partnerships were born and scrapped, the Business Growth Service was closed in 2015. But Cameron was indefatigable.

"You're responsible for the inspiration we all draw from the values that you hold. The values of enterprise, of graft," Cameron said to entrepreneurs at the launch of his Small Business Manifesto later that year. "I want it for the small business that works round the clock to build something, employ people and make a success ... who put their lives on the line for their family ... We have got a battle for the backbone of Britain."

It is all there. The Entrepreneurial Myth surges with the romantic rhetoric. The collective necessity for enterprise is firmly on the entrepreneur's shoulders. Small business owners are not just running businesses; they are responsible for inspiring the masses; responsible for changing the country; responsible for leading an entrepreneurial revolution. Sacrifice – time, life and family –

is expected in the battle for Britain's backbone. It is not just a well-written political speech surging to a crescendo. It is layered with a psychological drive to follow ancient rags-to-riches stories. Add the isolation, vitriol, exclusion and double binds of the Myth. Now ask the entrepreneur to pivot their business from service to product.

COOLER WINDS OF MAY (2016 TO PRESENT DAY)

The UK's May Government[121] assumed power following Cameron's Brexit-sparked resignation. By 2017, a 13.7% decline in the number of start-ups marked the first year-on-year decline since 2010;[122] the Centre for Entrepreneurs noted the day-to-day championing of entrepreneurs had become muted,[123] generating an increasingly unfavourable environment for entrepreneurs.

It is impossible to separate May's premiership from the tragedy or opportunity – depending whether you are a Remainer or Brexiteer – of the UK's decision to leave the European Union. May's government responded with a flagship policy, Start-up Visas, due to be implemented in 2019, to streamline the visa process for entrepreneurs and invite a much wider demographic to set up businesses in the UK. She also sanctioned a new government-backed fund to provide easier access to capital for successful start-ups in need of investment for growth. The Patient Capital Programme was a "new £2.5 billion programme designed to enable long-term investment in high growth potential companies led by ambitious entrepreneurs who want to build successful, world-class businesses."

But much is unknown and uncertainty constrains business. Entrepreneurial leaps may have been inhibited by ambiguity about the deal with the EU, the unsettling immigration debate about available labour and the unchartered territory of the UK's trade relations with the rest of the world. Brexit uncertainty increases economic pressure on the UK and much depends on the final Brexit deal. The Governor of the Bank of England, Mark Carney, scored apocalyptic headlines[124] stating a so-called no-deal Brexit might cause the pound to slide and prompt house prices to fall by as much as 35%. Carney's stress test wasn't a prediction; it was doomsday modelling to test the robustness of the financial system. The upside, lost in panic, was that a good deal with the EU might release demand stifled by current ambiguity. Investment might surge with a significant boost to the economy.

The reality of Brexit will settle beyond this book – where do you think your business will be in five years' time? Schumpeter urged you to expect the unexpected; he warned you of the inherent instability of markets. It is perhaps a good thing that economists, politicians and entrepreneurs are comfortable predicting the future and trading the unknown.

Stateside, Donald Trump's[125] protectionist policies and the 45th president's combative style have horrified and delighted in equal measure. Small business remains the engine of growth as the Trump administration attempts to "usher in a new era of American prosperity ... giving more Americans the opportunity to start, scale, and succeed in businesses of their own." Aggressive tax cuts and investment initiatives have been introduced and business confidence has reached a 45-year high. The National Federation of Independent Businesses (NFIB) reports more growth, profit and jobs.[126] "Business is booming. As the tax and regulatory landscape changed, so did small business expectations and plans," said NFIB President and CEO Juanita Duggan. "We're now seeing the tangible results of those plans as small businesses report historically high, some record breaking, levels of increased sales, investment, earnings and hiring."

Of course, the quality and *equality* of growth matters too. And there is much to do. McKinsey Global Institute's 2016 gender parity report, for example, revealed that if the US unlocked the economic potential of women in work, it could add 0.8 of a point to annual GDP growth over the next decade.

In the US, the number of new businesses is increasing,[127] while the number of new jobs created by each new business is declining.[128] Only half of new businesses survive five years or longer.[129] Between 1993 and 2006, business churn increased, with greater numbers of businesses closing and starting up.[130] From 2007 onwards, there was a marked drop in US start-ups as business closures dominated. According to Harvard Business School cohort analysis,[131] more than 75% of early stage technology companies fail to return their investors capital or turn a profit. If considering tech-centric, venture capital backed start-ups, more than 90% still fail. And surviving the first few years is no guarantee of success: 50% of companies trading in year four eventually failed.

In the UK, data from the Office of National Statistics[132] analysed start-up survival between 2011 and 2016 – the most recent data available – and discovered 44.1% of businesses survived five years. The oft-quoted 90% failure rate can be sourced in the 2017 HM Treasury report[133] stating that only 10% of start-ups make it to a fourth round of investment. The 90% statistic is confirmed by

The Start-up Genome Project's analysis of over 3,200 high-growth tech start-ups. The Stanford/Berkeley collaboration sought to improve success rates and discovered that within three years, 92% of start-ups failed, of which 72% failed due to premature scaling. Do you think this is good enough? Where is your business?

Imagine the prize if these success statistics improved – even by a small margin. Imagine the contribution to your community, economy and life if your business is saved. Imagine this benefit multiplied globally.

CHAPTER 13.
ONE BOAT

Terminology like East, West, North and South, developed and developing, no longer describes the global condition.[134] Instead, there is a 'great convergence' of global norms, policy and business practice as the 88% of the world's population who live outside the West seek the living standards, (relative) peace and prosperity that most Western citizens have enjoyed over the past few decades.[135] This convergence is "one of the most powerful forces ever seen in human history," explains political economist Kishore Mahbubani. "For millennia, humanity as a whole had been divided by geography, history, religion, culture, verbal language and body language. Today, despite this rich residue of differences, we are converging on a certain set of norms on how to create better societies."[136]

Shared global norms include the acceptance of modern science, reliance on logical reasoning, a new social contract between those who rule and their people, and an increasing focus on multilateralism.[137] Critically, it is also increasingly the norm to embrace free-market economics as the only viable way to generate lasting prosperity. Herein enters the global entrepreneur.

Entrepreneurs set global ambitions and build global businesses. They personify enterprise, agency and prosperity. This drives radically different countries to pursue the same entrepreneurial ideals seen as the secret to the West's health and wealth. Globalization *needs* entrepreneurship to blend values, ideas, models, money and markets. Consequently, wherever you sit to read this book, you are bound with your entrepreneurial peers tens of thousands of miles away in China, or India, or the UK, or the US. You know it. Click the 'see translation' button on Instagram and read startling similar inspirational platitudes from your peers overseas.

As Mahbubani vividly describes, the global economy is no longer a flotilla of distinct, national interests. Instead, "the seven billion people who inhabit planet Earth ... live in 193 separate cabins on the same boat."[138] Examining enterprise policy in China and India illustrates the inescapable, intoxicating power of The Entrepreneurial Myth. It also serves as a vivid warning to economies who haven't yet fully crowned The Entrepreneur.

Is it possible to learn the hard lessons of damaged entrepreneurial mental health and needless business failure experienced in the West, so that the transitional economies enjoy a healthier prosperity?

This would involve developing a global understanding of The Entrepreneurial Myth. It would involve educators, legislators and entrepreneurs in China and India recognizing The Entrepreneurial Myth's misrepresentations and pivoting from its demands to create a new entrepreneurial narrative. First, consider China.

CHINA: 1980 TO PRESENT DAY

Deng Xiaoping[139] is widely credited as the chief architect of China's economic reform. China was impoverished and isolated following Mao's disastrous politics; Deng instigated an ambitious programme to increase foreign investment and fuel domestic growth. Constrained by communist ideology, free market competition was carefully boxed in Special Economic Zones. Initially established in the 1980s in coastal cities, later evolving into high-tech development zones, these economic development zones were a discreet way for the Communist Party of China (CPC) to experiment with market-orientated reforms.[140]

In the 1980s, enterprise was reluctantly regarded as a "necessary and useful supplement to the public sector."[141] As Deng worked to define "socialism with Chinese characteristics",[142] there was a doubling in the number of private firms.[143] Deng's deeply conservative colleague, Chen Yun, named the result a "birdcage economy"; a system airy enough to sustain the market, but with bars to keep control.

There were undoubtedly mixed messages about enterprise. Working for a private business was often stigmatized as lacking the security and prestige of state employment;[144] party officials who became private businessmen were said to have "jumped into the sea".[145] This was settled, in part, by Deng's 'Southern Tour' when he insisted policy makers should not ask whether a policy is socialist or capitalist but instead consider whether it serves to advance China's economy.[146] A number of government officials – nicknamed the 'gang of 1992' – subsequently started their own businesses and promoted the rapid expansion of private enterprise and direct foreign investment in these areas.

Not all credit Deng as an economist. "He has never said anything original about economics or economic policy," said one critic.[147] "[His] relatively infrequent discussions of economic matters ... are usually either very broad generalities, or simple restatement of points made by others." Slow economic change during Deng's presidency may be attributed to the demands of pro-democracy unrest[148] and the churn of globalization. Deng's party offered its people an implicit bargain: greater freedom in economic activities in exchange for less freedom in political life and increasingly restrictive media censorship. "The Party and the people were now facing in opposite directions," explains author Evan Osnos.[149] "Chinese society was becoming more diverse, raucous, and freewheeling, and the Party was becoming more homogenous, buttoned-down, and conservative."

It wasn't until 1997, under the presidency of Paramount Leader Jiang Zemin,[150] that private enterprise was given legal parity with the public sector[151] and there was an explicit policy to "control the big, while releasing the small". This meant that while large enterprises remained under tight state control, new flexible policies were adopted to free small enterprises. This didn't work well initially; there were major job losses as private enterprise struggled to absorb the millions of workers released from state employment.[152] Government and business were co-dependent. The government controlled more of the economy than statistics suggested by designating regulation and competition; determining land purchases, bank loans and stock market listing requirements. Political connections determined business survival and growth. Conversely, with most state-owned companies in decline, private sector tax payments were increasingly critical for government.

Attitudes to enterprise edged further forward with the formal incorporation of private ownership into the Chinese Constitution[153] in 1999 and China's membership of the World Trade Organization two years later.

This enterprise policy represents vast social change. Deng's reforms helped create the world's newest superpower from the world's largest authoritarian state.[154] One generation buried their wealth in the garden to avoid the political persecution of the Cultural Revolution; the next surpassed the US as the world's largest consumer of luxury goods. One generation endured 'thought reform' to correct individualistic thinking; the next flocked to study in European and American universities and returned home with Western qualifications and aspirations. One generation abhorred free-market fundamentalism; the next drove through some of its most basic ideas. And at the heart of this change stands The Entrepreneur.

The result has been a burgeoning middle class, improved living standards and a curious "redistribution of hope".[155] While 87% of Chinese, 50% of Brazilians and 45% of Indians think their country is going in the right direction; only 31% of Britons and 30% of Americans do. "The greatest improvements in history have occurred in the past 30 years, coinciding with the decision of China and India to open up and reform their economies in 1979 and 1991 respectively," concludes Mahbubani.[156] "As a result of their opening up of the world's two most populous countries, a staggering number of people are seeing their living standards improve."

This has implications for each and every country. Goldman Sachs[157] forecast that by 2050 or earlier, the number one and number two economies in the world will be China's and India's. The two countries have an unresolved border dispute and were on opposite sides of the Cold War, but they share a commitment to economic liberalisation and global integration. While the US-China relationship may be one of the most important geopolitical relationships today, that between China and India will be the most important one tomorrow. So, what happened in India in 1991?

INDIA: 1991 TO PRESENT DAY

Between the first Micro, Small and Medium Enterprises development organization (MSME) in the 1950s, and the start of Pamulaparti Venkata Narasimha Rao's tenure as India's Prime Minister, interest grew in the potential benefits of a competitive open market. Forty years and 11 prime ministers – particularly Rajiv Ghandi's capital-goods import 'reforms by stealth'[158] – laid the foundation for free-market reforms. These included commercial bank lending programmes, government procurement initiatives and new skills transfer training centres. The creation of Small Industries Development Bank of India as the principal bank for the MSME sector in 1990 was also significant; for the first time, advice and mentorship supplemented credit.

But 1991 was the watershed; India liberalized its economy in response to a growing economic crisis and highly uncompetitive domestic markets. Import controls were dismantled, customs duties slashed, licensing liberalized and capital markets opened up. Two years later, the Delayed Payment Act empowered MSMEs to charge interest on late payments. The reforms boosted entrepreneurial activity and growth rates climbed steadily to 6%[159] in the 1990s.

Reform to competition laws and social security regulations for workers in the so-called 'unorganized sector' progressed. A credit guarantee scheme was introduced to mitigate personal risk shouldered by entrepreneurs. Then, the MSME Development Act 2006 was ratified[160] and the MSME Ministry established. These activities consolidated a decade's reform; for the first time, the concept of enterprise had a legal framework in India.

In 2014, Prime Minister Narendra Modi was elected on a platform of increasing job creation, wider economic reform and improving infrastructure to revive economic growth. "The only solution to every problem is economic development without which India's destiny will not change," he declared.[161] A charismatic politician and an instinctive supporter of small business, Modi unwittingly leveraged The Entrepreneurial Myth with rags-to-riches tales of his rise from a street tea seller. He vowed government would play the role of facilitator,[162] not master. Nevertheless, the economy initially slowed during his tenure. Demonetization – where Modi declared 86% of India's cash defunct to tackle 'black money' – undoubtedly hurt micro businesses by stripping out informal cash flow. It also hurt Modi's credibility; critics questioned his translation of principle to policy.[163]

Renewed focus on the bureaucratic business environment helped boost India's ranking in the World Bank's Ease of Doing Business Report[164] but entrepreneurs continued to cite corruption and inadequate infrastructure as business limitations. New initiatives persisted: *Make in India* for the manufacturing sector, *Stand-Up India*[165] for female entrepreneurs, and *Start-up India*[166] with its branded combination of research parks and incubators, funding and mentoring.

The reward has been robust growth. The most recent International Monetary Fund forecast[167] for India's GDP growth 2017-18 is 7.3% as a result of strengthening investment and healthy domestic consumption. Medium-term growth prospects, helped by ongoing structural reforms, are forecast at a heady 7.75%. Compare this with world growth forecasts of 3.7% and China's growth forecast of 6.6%.

For better or worse, entrepreneurs lead this growth. India's Sixth Economic Census recorded 58.5 million business establishments, of which 96.4% were privately owned and nearly 72% sole traders (or 'own account establishments').[168] The growth of the nation rests on the shoulders of tens of millions of entrepreneurs. Their impact is felt throughout India. Growth in numbers of self-employed in India is linked to 10% growth in annual income for the bottom 20% of the population.[169] At the other end of the pay spectrum, graduates from the Indian Institute of Technology (IIT) make remarkable contributions in Silicon Valley or major Western corporations.[170] IIT alumni entrepreneurs include N. R. Narayana Murthy (cofounder and former chairman of Infosys), Rajendra S. Pawar (cofounder and chairman of NIIT), Vinod Khosla (cofounder of Sun Microsystems), Anurag Dikshit (cofounder of PartyGaming), and Suhas S. Patil (founder of Cirrus Logic). These entrepreneurial stars sponsor others; Khosla is now a venture capitalist investing over $1 billion in other businesses.

India's digital economy and business process outsource industry has earnt the country the title of 'the world's back office'[171] and spurred new waves of entrepreneurship, complete with home-grown unicorns. Such unicorns, or tech start-ups valued at more than $1 billion, include e-commerce player Flipkart, ride-hailing company Ola Cabs and mobile ad platform inMobi. India's tech sector has grown from around $2.5 billion in the late 1990s to more than $100 billion in 2016.[172] Challenges from tech automation and US protectionism lie ahead[173] as the country grapples with sustaining growth and distributing wealth.

ONE MYTH

So, what does this tour of global enterprise policy tell you? There is no conspiracy to withhold the support businesses need to survive and grow. Society benefits from entrepreneurial wealth; communities need the jobs created by entrepreneurial businesses. Governments in the UK, the US, China and India duly attempt to harness the next prosperous wave of creative destruction with initiative and legislation. Governments want business to work.

As argued by the indefatigable Lord Digby Jones, former minister for UK trade and investment, business is the sole generator of taxation revenue for the country.[174] "When a Business makes money there are only three things it can do with the profit," he reasons. "Reward the shareholders who took the risk by way of dividend or capital gain on sale, and the shareholder will pay tax on it. Or keep the profit in the business and pay tax on it. Or pay employees – who'll pay tax on it! The tax goes in part to pay the wages of people in the public sector – who'll pay tax on it! If it wasn't for the wealth created by businesses across the land, large and small, there would be no tax, there would be no public sector." Enterprise fuels global economies. Work, works. Governments craft just enough policy to nudge the entrepreneur and the free market into action.

But there is a problem: not creative destruction, but creative distraction.

CHAPTER 14.
CREATIVE DISTRACTION

If you review the enterprise policies of the UK, the US, India and China, you can identify a distinct bias towards The Entrepreneur of The Entrepreneurial Myth. Policy is predisposed towards nurturing the special solo inventor, pen poised, waiting for inspiration to strike. Then, *Eureka!* A quick sketch, a willing supply chain and happy global customers. Difficult, slow, messy, real business can't compete. The Entrepreneurial Myth is so pervasive, so intoxicating, it distracts politicians from the enterprise policy desperately needed by the majority of business protagonists. It skews resulting enterprise policy in three core ways. The Entrepreneurial Myth encourages:

1. Short-term politically expedient policy, not a long-term vision and support required by most businesses;
2. Manufacturing enterprise initiatives, not policy designed to nurture the majority of service-sector businesses; and
3. Start-up enterprise initiatives, not policy designed to support business at predictable scale-up hurdles.

1. SHORT-TERM POLITICS VERSUS LONG-TERM BUSINESS

A short parliamentary or presidential term forces politicians to make a choice. The years required to carefully craft a reputation based on honesty and integrity competes with the spin and soundbite of a quick-fix initiative. Evan Davis, in his pithy analysis *Post-Truth: Peak Bullshit*,[175] calls this the dismal cycle: "in order to be there for the long term, [politicians] have to survive the short term which makes the short term the only period that matters." The only election that matters is the next election.[176] It would take a long time to design and deliver an enterprise programme reflecting the blood, sweat and tears of real business. And it's psychologically uncomfortable to wait. The political horizon is just too short. Imagine you are faced with the choice between influence now, or integrity in the future. What would you really do?

It is easier and quicker to pass responsibility for wealth creation to the entrepreneur: "we got you going, off you go, now deliver the economic benefits we need." A start-up initiative is short, sharp and shiny. It is a gesture that speaks volumes. It signals the government is serious about creating employment – yet has been proved not to sustain employment. The entrepreneur doesn't just carry the message, he is the message; the personification of enterprise. Long-term prosperity and entrepreneurial mental health are unwittingly traded for short-term political careerism.

2. MANUFACTURING SECTOR VERSUS SERVICES SECTOR

As countries grow, they tend to evolve from the sweat of agriculture, to blue-collar manufacturing, to deindustrialised white-collar services in business, retail and finance. As people move from fields, to factories, to offices and stores, they earn more and spend more. The country enjoys a virtuous cycle of health, wealth and well-being as living standards improve. This evolution seems inevitable, irreversible and, most importantly, desirable. Yet the financial crisis revealed the dark side of a financial-service sector peddling impenetrable, intangible products. Sometimes, you need a master's degree to understand what is sold by a financier or lawyer or consultant. You can't box it, count it and stack it on a shelf. So, there is a political push to rebalance the economy from services to manufacturing. In his 2011 budget speech, George Osborne urged business to do just that: the UK needed a manufacturing revival to redress the economy's imbalance. But this is notoriously difficult to do.

While enterprise policy makers claim their support is sector-agnostic, it's harder to tailor policy to support service businesses as opposed to manufacturing.[177] First, how can you measure value delivered in an hour's conversation versus the production of a widget? How can you increase the productivity or efficiency of that hour? Author, journalist and academic Linda Yueh rightly points to businesses that straddle both sectors: Rolls Royce, for example, makes more money maintaining its engines than selling them, yet sits firmly in the manufacturer category. So, categorization and measurement is an issue. Second, aptitude. The UK and other developed economies are particularly good at providing high margin services such as legal, accountancy, advertising and management consultancy. Third, globalization. It is harder for rich nations to recapture the infrastructure needed to competitively manufacture goods. Information technology has lowered the cost of logistics, while multilateral agreements to reduce trade tariffs and remove restrictive practices liberate lower-cost producers. All three factors resist the return to manufacturing.

Unsurprisingly, neither the UK nor the US economy has managed the shift from services.[178] Britain's services sector has recovered to pre-recession levels, while manufacturing has not. Britain's trade deficit – the difference between the value of imported and exported goods and services – hit a record high in the years following 2008. It's all relative, of course; Britain remains the ninth-biggest manufacturer in the world and the US remains the second biggest.[179] The intangible products of the service sector – a sector which dominates start-up statistics – may explain why the entrepreneur becomes the personification of enterprise policy. And they are between a rock and a hard place.

There is tension between political preference for manufacturing and makers, and service-orientated enterprise policy. There is a gentle contradiction at the heart of economic and political staging with the potential to heighten The Entrepreneurial Myth's impact.

3. START-UP VERSUS SCALE-UP

Start-up is sexy. Start-up is hot-desking, blue-sky thinking and constant cappuccino drinking. It's the pensive cool of Shoreditch or downtown Brooklyn, not the entitled shout of London's Square Mile or Manhattan. Herein lies the problem. Politics, cruelly labelled show business for ugly people, desperately needs the glamour of a tech hub. It needs the optimism and potential of a start-up. Subsequently, hundreds of enterprise initiatives cluster in those intoxicating first years of business creation hoping that The Entrepreneurial Myth's magic will rub off on them.

But just as a teenager needs more of you than a toddler, so *scale-up* businesses need funds, support and guidance. If you know a business owner who has survived the first three years, call them, ask them what they need; free office space and coffee won't cut it.

Yet political assumptions skew the division of resources between start-up and scale-up sectors.

Small business is conflated with high growth and high returns, when there is no systematic relationship between size and growth. "While many high-growth firms are small, many small firms are not high growth," Mazzucato[180] reminds us. "The bursts of rapid growth that promote innovation and create employment are often staged by firms that have existed for several years and grown incrementally until they reached a take-off stage. This is a major problem since so many government policies focus on tax breaks and benefits to SMEs, with the aim of making the economy more innovative and productive." Smaller businesses also have a higher attrition rate, wasting valuable start-up resources. Some economies that have favoured SMEs have performed worse.[181]

At the same time, scale-up businesses are assumed to be a more labour-intensive investment requiring significant non-financial nurturing and coaching. Consequently, scale-ups are rigorously screened. Thus, despite potentially being a safer bet than those in the start-up sector, fewer businesses are selected to receive the scale-up support they need.

"Every government has limited resources. By trying to help the small companies, I wonder if we inadvertently disincentivise growth," admits Keiller, formerly Chairman of Scottish Enterprise. "If you give every small business an allowance, does that put people off wanting to be a bigger business? As soon as you trigger VAT or rates, it's much less fun and much more bureaucratic. The profit margin goes down. Perhaps it's easier to stay small?

"And from an economic perspective, there is an argument that we should spend more on scale-ups. By nature, this is more selective. If spending is more focused, fewer people get benefit, more are excluded. There is a maturity needed to say: this isn't a freebie, handout or a lottery. Prove you are in a place where you are willing to grow and able to make a difference to the economy by providing jobs. Prove this is ultimately something that will pay mountains of corporation tax back into the exchequer – wherever that exchequer happens to be – and you'll create high paid jobs for people who will spend their wages in the local economy."

Start-up versus scale-up dilemmas ultimately erode the efficiency and effectiveness of support.

US business leader Jim Alampi[182] believes small business growing pains are predictable. His research indicates that businesses meet challenges and barriers to growth at the following points:

1. Revenue reaches $1 million or you employ more than ten people;
2. Revenue reaches $10 million or you employ between 50 and 75 people;
3. Revenue reaches $50 million or you employ between 200 and 400 people;

4. Revenue reaches $500 million or you employ over 1,000 people.

Alampi believes barriers appear in three predictable areas: leadership, infrastructure and market dynamics. As a business matures, the requirements for leaping over each of these barriers changes. Knowing where the barriers are – and bracing your business as you approach the hurdle – is the difference between a failed start-up and a sustainable business that survives and flourishes for generations.[183] The start-up begins with one or two people and an idea; it is exciting, all-consuming but chaotic. As employees and customers are added to the business, functional systems have to evolve. You need an organization chart; then middle management. Jack-of-all-trades has to specialise and become a master-of-one. A new eye is required for quality, customers, finance and data. The options are stark; adapt or die.

The gritty hard work of growth is invisible to most; it takes place at your kitchen table in the small hours and tests the patience of your family with another weekend in the office. The stretch required to clear Alampi's hurdles challenges The Entrepreneurial Myth's mantra that business is easy. And the slog required to adapt and grow isn't politically attractive. Consider the enterprise initiatives launched in the UK and the US over the past 50 years; start-up trumps scale-up. Speech writers and policy makers seem to prefer the quick-fix gloss of a new business incubator.

CHAPTER 15.
THE PROFESSOR'S REPLY

Alistair R. Anderson is the Distinguished Professor of Entrepreneurship at Lancaster University in the UK. He also holds various honorary and visiting professor roles including, SLU in Sweden, Audencia Business School in France, RGU in Scotland, University of Tehran in Iran and University of Peradeniya in Sri Lanka. "Whilst there is much to admire in entrepreneurship, this admiration has created a mythological all-conquering hero," agrees Anderson. "It seems the eulogy of praise and social appreciation has created a culture where being enterprising generates social esteem. The pervasion is such that it's not just the alert business folk or sharp-eyed dealers who stake a claim for the role; bureaucrats and even universities feel entitled to a share of the associated prestige.

"But the adulation diminishes when it becomes clear that most entrepreneurs share our own human frailties. They make mistakes, sometimes big mistakes, they are fallible and have no special insights into what the future will hold. Part of the de-bunking or, if you prefer, understanding of the character is that many simply want to make a living on their own terms. Just like the rest of us. Yet, in my view, it is these very human qualities and behaviours that we should admire in our entrepreneurs.

"Most new businesses fail or cease in the first few years. This is because it is very difficult indeed to build a sustainable new business. This is the biggest problem with The Entrepreneurial Myth. It is so powerful that people believe, and are encouraged, they 'can do it too'. Yet the determination, hard work and sheer grind is overlooked, overwhelmed by the tidal wave of this powerful cultural expectation. We should admire these qualities, particularly for the few who succeed, but especially for those who fail and get up and try again.

"Moreover, the benefits of entrepreneurship can hardly be over-stated. Economically, entrepreneurs are part of a great natural experiment. They each try out new products and services. Those that work, benefit our economy, creating jobs and wealth. For those that fail, they carry the total cost of trying. It costs us nothing; it is almost as if we freeride on their efforts. Entrepreneurial failure is part of an economic process that ignores the personal cost to small businesses. The power of the Myth lies in the portrayal of entrepreneurs as masters of change, while in reality change is a fickle mistress. Sometimes it works out, sometimes it doesn't.

"But there is more to entrepreneurship than wealth creation. Becoming master of your own destiny is a remarkable achievement. The satisfaction may even sweeten the bitterness of failure – *at least I tried*. There is the confidence that this role can liberate; a new but substantive status and meaning to those discriminated against because of gender or colour. The power of entrepreneurs has also been turned to social value creation; we now see social enterprising improving disadvantaged lives.

"We can see the constitution of our Entrepreneurial Myth and the mythmakers. We understand how we got caught up in a storm of uncertainties and how entrepreneurs seemed the only ones capable of leading us out of the turbulence. We know now that entrepreneurship is one route, a good one, but needs skilled navigators and decent maps, not just enthusiasm. We are no longer dazzled by the Myth so must make better judgements about what we admire and how much we should praise these heroes of the modern age."

IN BRIEF:
ECONOMICS

- Two grandfathers of modern economics – Adam Smith and Joseph Schumpeter – introduced the entrepreneur as the source of economic growth.
- A timeline of UK and US enterprise policy traces the entrepreneur's role change from job creator, to recession rescuer, to equality warrior, to the nation's inspiration.
- Radically different countries – the UK, the US, China, India – pursue the same entrepreneurial ideals as globalization blends interests. There is one Entrepreneurial Myth with global reach. There may be an opportunity for transitional economies to enjoy a healthier entrepreneurial prosperity.
- The Entrepreneurial Myth encourages short-term politically expedient policy, not the long-term vision and support required by most businesses.
- The Entrepreneurial Myth encourages manufacturing enterprise initiatives, not policy designed to nurture the majority of service sector businesses.

- The Entrepreneurial Myth encourages start-up enterprise initiatives, not policy designed to support business at predictable scale-up hurdles.
- There is an opportunity to develop a more effective, more reflective, entrepreneurship.

You have heard the case to recalibrate entrepreneurship; to rid business creation of its puff and myth. But what now?

The irrepressible human drive to explore, create and trade remains. The need to have a go, to make it better, to start again, remains. The economic compulsion to trade goods and trade up remains. Here is the opportunity to relish real business with its mess and mistakes, griefs and glories. It is time to listen to real business creators; meet four entrepreneurs and a wild card:

- Dean Hunter (Chapter 18) was part of a team that secured a billion-dollar deal but he developed his second business with a radically different model. He led this business through oil crash and recession to growth by giving 30% away. Hear why the game show exit doesn't exist and the power of being frank.
- Psychotherapist Colin Brett (Chapter 19) lost it all before building a successful international business coaching thousands of entrepreneurs. Join him to reflect on who you might be as you step out from The Entrepreneurial Myth's shadow.
- Colin O'Donnell (Chapter 20) is a seasoned tech entrepreneur who sold his business to a Google subsidiary and now nurtures a new moonshot project. He realized that illusive Silicon Valley tech dream. The Myth would frame Colin's success as easy genius, but instead hear the untold story of operators and team heroes.

- Lora Fachie (Chapter 22) has just started her entrepreneurial journey and launched her first business following golden Paralympian success. She experienced crushing trackside failure to fight back and win gold at the Rio 2016 Paralympic Games. You are invited to think about success as she does.
- Wildcard Gretchen Haskins (Chapter 21) isn't an entrepreneur, but her compelling story of leading aviation safety offers real business creators a unique opportunity. You are invited to think of failure – more importantly, think of performance – as she does.

TAKE ACTION.

THE REAL BUSINESS MANIFESTO

CHAPTER 16.
MIND THE GAP

The definition of entrepreneurship remains so stubbornly broad, it can be meaningless. Remember Gartner's "generic 'everyman'"?[184] He's Richard, Elon, Jack; but also that woman selling soap door to door, also that self-employed dreamer in the coffee shop. Entrepreneurship is more than ambition, intellect and will, more than innovation. Entrepreneurs create opportunity and opportunity sparks hope. Hope captivates us all.

In this space, The Entrepreneurial Myth does its damage. It is the chasm between the puffed-up, all-powerful, economic saviour found in business schools, media and enterprise policy, and the gritty reality of launching and running a small business. There is a world between the Silicon Valley stars and the 58.5 million anonymous entrepreneurs propping up India's economy. New labels distract further. Founders, creators, opportunists, sole traders, multi-hyphenates – yet all are subject to the same entrepreneurial mythmaking trap.

The Entrepreneurial Myth is so pervasive, it is almost invisible. The 30-year media analysis at the heart of this book pricks the Myth's rhetoric and drags it into the light. You can see it clearly now.

- The Myth distorts business success. It says: business is easy, follow this man, just ten top tips to wealth and wisdom!
- Money follows the Myth, so diverse talent is systematically excluded from real business.
- The Myth can isolate business protagonists by minimising real business struggles.
- There is potentially evidence – though much more research is needed – that the Myth jeopardizes or justifies disproportionate mental health problems in entrepreneurs.
- The Myth inspires, perhaps excuses, enterprise policy inadvertently focused on manufacturing, not services; skewed to start-up, not scale-up; for short-term politics, not long-term wealth generation.

The glittering multi-billion contribution made by entrepreneurial grafters means this uncertainty, risk and damage is tolerated. You tolerate The Entrepreneurial Myth for its addictive instant hit of adoration. Until now, perhaps you didn't spot the Myth's hangover of self-loathing when you stand with the 90% of start-ups that fail. Deep down, despite the top tips podcasts in your ear and the Branson biography by your bed, you know the answer isn't in your guts. The honest answer to wealth, health and success lies elsewhere.

It's time to change.

This book proposes you look up from your entrepreneurial gut – brilliant though it may be – and share enterprise with a supportive community of talents. This book proposes education and legislation pivots to meet real business priorities. It proposes that the adoring myth-making of those at the top is tempered with real stories, without the needy whine for a happy ending.

Let's pool the isolated whispers of entrepreneurial struggle to form a shout of support for those in the tough, messy middle. Let's rely on camaraderie with real peers; not complicity with a mythical guru. Entrepreneurs are already prodigious networkers. But how dark and dangerous, how *authentic*, is the conversation?

It's time to change the conversation.

- The truth exposes The Entrepreneurial Myth. This is the manifesto pledge to SPEAK. Speak up, be frank, listen hard, be well.
- If you are not the entrepreneur of the Myth, who are you? And who do you want to be next? This is the manifesto pledge to REFLECT. Reflect, be brave, learn the lesson, start again.
- Where is your collective? And how will you reach them? This is the manifesto pledge to CONNECT. Discover your purpose, find your tribe, share talents and teams.
- This is the manifesto pledge to LEARN. Think about business failure like an aviator.
- This is the manifesto pledge to PERSIST. Think about business success like an athlete.

There is a yawning gap between the mythical Entrepreneur promoted through education, politics and media

– and the messy, fallible, real thing. This gap – The Entrepreneurial Myth – damages real business creators by jeopardizing entrepreneurial mental well-being; it damages our economies and societies as it persuades the public and politicians to accept, even celebrate, appalling business failure rates. Essential business talent is excluded, policy is skewed, attitudes to success and failure distorted. All this is to the detriment of our economies.

Real entrepreneurial business still offers exhilarating roller-coaster chaos; it remains as unapologetically brutal as it is intoxicating. You would do it all over again.

Just, this time, you can mind the gap.

CHAPTER 17.
KEEP IT TOGETHER

Humanistic psychology is built on the philosophical scaffolding of Socrates and Sartre, Heidegger and Binswanger. It was a mid-century retort to Freud's psychoanalysis and Skinner's behaviourism. You are more than a brain in a body reacting to the environment, it says. Your meaning is not determined by those unresolved issues with your mother. Instead, you are creative, resourceful and whole. You have incredible untapped potential. You can choose for yourself. That's why you feel that nagging striving to self-actualize and be the very best version of yourself.

Carl Rogers was humanistic psychology's favourite son. He studied the experience of experience; not just the churn of sensory data but the processes you live through, imagination, thought, language, emotion and action. Your subjective experience *is* your world, said Rogers. You have absolute autonomy and you have phenomenal potential. Humanistic psychology believes the human experience rests on three pillars:[185] freedom of will (you can do what you want), the will to meaning (you crave a life that makes sense and makes an impact) and the meaning of life (you want the world to mean something too). You strive for an "unconditional faith in unconditional meaning".[186] It is *purpose* – not the Freudian pleasure or Nietzschean power – that propels you through the world.

But beware of narcissism. Humanistic psychologies start with the self, work on the self, reward the self, to fulfil the self. Self-care, self-love, self-centred. The Entrepreneurial Myth's narrow avatars of success – the billionaire in jeans or the tech philanthropist – seem the ultimate in self-actualized celebrity-endorsed self-development. There is also a rabbit hole of relativism: your truth suits you, mine suits me, my truth has changed today, surely all can coexist?

You know truth when you encounter it. There are absolutes – not just an individual introspective exercise constructing something that feels like truth. There is a reality beyond you and your immediate understanding; a gift you can't control. You stand on solid ground. While there is autonomy and potential, there is also community and responsibility, belief and faith, right and wrong. So, if your best version of you is an impossible Myth, step back to see the universal horizon line.

Heartfelt disclaimer aside, let's join the pragmatists. While there is much wrong with this model or that model, much remains valid and good. Clinicians from radically different schools usually pick 'what works' based on clinical experience, intuition, common sense and reflection without a reconciliatory therapeutic school of thought. So, whatever your philosophical position, imagine the taut psychological space between who you think you are, who you want to be, who others think you are and who you really are. A good life is defined by thoughtfully, gently, pinching this gap closed. This means to live a life as *congruently* – to use Rogers' term – as possible. When you do this, daring, creativity, adaptability, tolerance and spontaneity flourish. You are living well. "This process of the good life is not, I am convinced, a life for the faint-hearted," Rogers reminds us. "It involves the stretching and growing of becoming more and more of one's poten-tialities. It involves the courage to be. It means launching oneself fully into the stream of life."[187]

The flipside is true. It is risky to ignore or fuel the gap between who you think are, who you want to be, what others think and the reality of your talents. Indulge The Entrepreneurial Myth by chasing an illusory entrepre-neurial life and misery follows. It is essential you mind your gap to pursue and preserve health, wealth and hap-piness. The truth exposes The Entrepreneurial Myth, so first consider the manifesto pledge to SPEAK.

CHAPTER 18.
SPEAK

REALITY CHECK

Dean Hunter was part of an entrepreneurial team who initiated a management buy-out of a global energy company and successfully sold the business five years later for $955 million. He subsequently launched and built his own market-leading consultancy delivering commercial human resources to hundreds of leaders and entrepreneurial businesses in over 20 sectors. "You need to be honest about your point and purpose. I have worked with hundreds of entrepreneurs and their businesses. Many are driven by an innate 'I'm not good enough'," explains Hunter over a chilled glass of wine. "Many come from a poor background or a background that wasn't very loving. There is an insatiable hunger to prove something time and time again. They won't tell you but if you look hard you can see the insecurity.

"I know; I set up my business to create financial security for my daughter. I was once asked how much I needed to be secure. At that time, it was in the millions, but nobody needs millions to survive! Money is a smoke-screen. I've questioned my purpose over the years when I've run businesses in recession and peak markets. When you are running a business in recession, you have to have a good reason and clear purpose to get out of bed and keep going. Money is just not enough.

"You need a reality check about setting up your own business. I set my own business up having worked 70 hours a week for 15 years in the energy sector. I wanted work-life balance. I intended to work on my own but within 12 months, I had 30 staff and perhaps 100 clients. You believe you're going to work for yourself but in reality, you have 100 demanding bosses.

"You need a reality check about the deal. As a consultant, I've sat with entrepreneurs facing the worst thing they can imagine – business failure. They are wrestling with shame because, in their eyes, they haven't proved they are good enough. They have spent 20 years building a business and now it's gone. Their purpose has gone. Yet over that 20-year period, thousands of people enjoyed a job, career opportunities and development. They built something valued and loved. How often does somebody stand up to say: 'I created this business, I thought I was going to retire, it fell apart, but this is what I learned, here I am.' There is no middle ground, just failure, hidden away in these conversations.

"I've been there myself. I remember sitting in my back garden when the oil price crashed in 2015, shaking, thinking I have to stop paying 70 people's salaries. These people are like my brothers and sisters and family. I was exhausted but kept going and going until my team knocked on my door. They said: 'we want to take over the running of the business and we think we're ready.' It was the toughest decision and the best decision. We do need more to stand up and say: 'I'm an entrepreneur, I struggle.' Or to say: 'I didn't get my payday, but this is what I learned.' It's like a coming out and takes time. Changing the conversation is difficult. Sometimes it takes a life event, a moment, for someone to see it for themselves. It takes a board, a coach, someone who cares, to hold the mirror up.

"The first step is recognition that it's not just you. You're not alone. Your success or failure belongs to your team too. My employees own 30% of my business for this reason. We're all in it together; we all survive and thrive, or we all fail together. Employee ownership automatically changes your purpose. We share ownership, we share responsibility. We share the pain and gain. And I have a managing director who holds the mirror up to me, who checks my behaviours and cares about the whole of me. She gives me perspective. It's not all or nothing; it's not deal or no deal. There doesn't need to be a deal in 18 months or five years or at all. And the hard work has paid off. We are back to 100% growth per annum and doing very, very well.

"Entrepreneurs think of the deal to exit their business as if it was a game show. 'I am going to do this for a few years, I'm going to sell it and then I'm going to lie on the beach with a cocktail.' But nobody will ever value your business as you do. While it's your child, it's a commodity for the acquirer, it's a means of achieving their strategy. We become a bit entitled when we create a business. We think we deserve our pay out. But, actually, do we? Products and services go out of fashion. Staff leave and make your business vulnerable. We're not entitled to anything. The game show prize is not a contractual right. I can't see it written down anywhere.

"Imagine if we considered the jobs, careers and many years of development and experience generated by our businesses as enough. What then?"

This book has dragged The Entrepreneurial Myth into the light to show you how this punchy social construct might influence individual business creators and our economies. You have witnessed the Myth marauding through the business landscape, excluding diverse talent, distorting ideas of success and failure, isolating business protagonists, demonizing weakness and jeopardizing entrepreneurial mental health. You have seen how the Myth distracts policy makers so entrepreneurs who need long-term, scale-up, service-sector backing – the majority – aren't supported as well as they might be.

But as with every social construct, you bear some responsibility for The Entrepreneurial Myth's power. Remember the mental maps we need to organize life's chaos and data? This constructionist perspective explains how words create worlds and your brain generates experience. You have seen how The Entrepreneurial Myth is a powerful mental map shared by business creators, educators, legislators and politicians. Shared by you. Language is often inadequate so metaphor – the magical entrepreneurial superhero, modern Greek god and business guru – illustrates what you mean. Behaviour follows the stories shared. Remember, semiotics explains how everything you do, or don't do, crafts a message and creates meaning. You can't sit outside; you already sing in the chorus.

Although Davis writes of modern gibberish, obfuscation and spin, he could be speaking of The Entrepreneurial Myth when he advises the information we are fed is based on the information we choose to consume.[188]

There is no such thing as 'The Media',[189] just a mash of journalists cooperating, competing and conflicting with each other. Most are focused on what you want to hear. So, choose differently.

The Myth is as reliant on your elevator pitch and networking conversation as the pages of your favourite broadsheet. You create the Myth. Consider how entrepreneurs collude with the Myth in the curious names of their businesses and projects: consider, Golden Dreams, Phoenix and Gulliver; Alchemy, Cyclops and Gabriel. And we have all read a secular business 'bible'.[190] Ironically, journalists accuse entrepreneurs of lapping up the idolatry created.[191]

Consider also how the Myth gathers strength when you smile 'fine' to dismiss questions about business progress. It gathers strength when that pebble under your tongue stops you speaking honestly with your peers. You network with other entrepreneurs, of course, but the conversation follows defensive conventions. This turns peers into unwitting conspirators of the Myth. When you spin a bad month, or laugh at the recessionary climate with stories of triumph and success, entrepreneurial mythmaking soars and the gap widens.

There is evidence your reaction to the Myth influences your wellbeing, the health of your peers and ultimately the wealth of global economies. Your mythmaking matters. And herein lies your opportunity.

You already hold the power to deconstruct The Entrepreneurial Myth using the same language, understanding and behaviour that drew this map in the first place. You have an opportunity to change your words to create a world without The Entrepreneurial Myth. As proposed by sociologist Howard Becker,[192] words can become labels, can become social identity, can become a self-fulfilling prophesy. Change the words, change the outcome.

What would it be like to tell real, raw, stories of entrepreneurship without the psychological scaffolding of epic quests and rags to riches? Davis reminds us of how difficult, yet how essential, it is to "break out of the mindset of selling rather than simply telling."[193] What would it be like to authentically relate to your fellow entrepreneur without the relentless mythical sell? Imagine the relief of describing the dark corners of your business while your peer nods with understanding. Imagine that nagging fear is shared and silenced. Imagine the bright edge of celebration without the shadow of imposter syndrome.

And just as you control the words you use and the world you build, you control the point and purpose of your business. What if, just as Hunter proposes, the jobs, careers and experience of your business were enough without the glossy exit? Rand Fishkin calls for a "more middle-of-the-road start-up life cycle" in his Silicon Valley expose[194] as he rejects the dualism of 'go big or go home'. It is a decisive rejection of the game show deal and the illusion of an exit's "almost mystical sense of closure and accomplishment".

Contemplate Hunter's reality check. Take off the entrepreneurial mask. Remember that research revealing the psychological trade-off between the ferocious hard work and illusory entrepreneurial benefits? Ease away from self-justification and the stories you tell to make the sacrifice sound worth it. Learn a new business vocabulary that includes 'but', 'not too good' and 'help'. Change the conversation at the next networking event. Connect. Share what you think, what you really, really, think. Say: leading your business is harder than you ever thought, you're not sure you can do it. Say: it is relentless; it demands every waking hour. Say: everyone wants a piece of you but, perversely, you are alone. How hard it is to leave the sentiment there and resist the perky chirping of The Entrepreneurial Myth! That's the point. Rest assured, your inner monologue will resonate with others. Use it to connect honest stories, podcast whispers and entrepreneurial confessionals. Take them to your next meeting, write them into your performance report. See beyond the game show deal; hear what's beneath the bravado. Hold up your colleague's mirror, as they hold up yours. Neither celebrate nor denigrate stories of struggle. Instead, co-create an entrepreneurship wide enough and broad enough for failure. Normalize tiredness and a bad day. This book has framed The Entrepreneurial Myth and made sense of its power. Just as the coordinated campaigns and stories about mental health and wellbeing are slowly starting to reduce stigma,[195] so The Entrepreneurial Myth loses some of its power to distract and punish and shame when shared.

So: speak up, be frank, listen hard, be well. This takes courage, of course. Think of what you have to lose. If you are not the entrepreneur of the Myth, who are you? And who do you want to be next? Next, is the manifesto pledge REFLECT.

CHAPTER 19.
REFLECT

COURAGEOUS REFLECTION

Colin Brett has coached thousands of entrepreneurs and entrepreneurial organizations during his 40-year career in psychotherapy, counselling, training and coaching. He is an International Coach Federation (ICF) Professional Certified Coach, a Transactional Analyst and a qualified Neuro-linguistic Programming (NLP) trainer. Colin founded an international coach training business. "Humans need to belong to groups. Groups give us feedback and recognition, and we will do pretty much anything to get that recognition," smiles Brett as he settles into his chair. "But consider the conditions of belonging to a group like the entrepreneurial community. We mustn't break the rules; we must stoke the façade. We put on the suit and the smile and go to the networking meeting. We exchange marshmallow strokes; the conversation is pink, fluffy, looks splendid, tastes lovely, but is gone in a second. It's all colour and sugar. So, we return home and sit in front of the proposal and know we're dying inside.

No-one is looking after us behind the scenes. We're left with the hollowness, heaviness and angst. We haven't been heard or seen, touched or genuinely cared for. We lead a dual life.

"It's the Hawthorne Effect where we change our behaviour when we know we're being watched. If I believe I need to brag to get respect from you – and I really, really want your respect – then I'm only going to tell you the things I think you want to hear. What I learn as an entrepreneur is that the way for me to get recognition is to tell of a success that may or may not be true. Or I inflate my successes and play down what it cost me. It nearly cost me my sanity but I'm not going to tell you that.

"We find ourselves creating a reality that pleases others – peers, parents, politicians – but we are withering behind the façade. Depression follows because there is a dissonance – a clash, a gap – between who we try to be and who we feel we are. In the end, we fall into the hole.

"I did this grandly. I was married at 38, divorced at 40, I was ill and gave up my business. I had no resources. The old structures had gone. I lived through the absolute terror of having nothing left. There is a saying in German: *ist der Ruf erst ruiniert, dann lebt es sich ganz ungeniert*. In other words: when you have lost your reputation, there is nothing left to lose. When you lose what you think is really important and discover the loss makes no real difference, you can get on with the real thing.

"It takes courage to stop giving ourselves away, to stop sacrificing our wellbeing to external expectations. It takes courage to be who we are; to say, actually, what you want for me and what I've said I want for me, is no longer what's right for me.

"We goad ourselves on with the fear of failure. We live as if our beliefs that 'I'm only OK if I ...' were reality. But the opposite is true; you are OK as you are. So, decide to not put on the mask in the morning; decide to move away from the self-imposed 'should's'. The relief when we do that! We no longer feel driven. We have become real. We become free to be really creative.

"Entrepreneurs are known for their courage – so have the courage to be imperfect. Aim for what you want, rather than what you think other people want. Screw your courage to the sticking place.

"Ask yourself or, better still sit with a coach, and consider; what are you doing this for? *Who* are you doing this for? Where are *you* in your business? What do you want? How will you achieve this in a way that isn't going to cost you your life or sanity or health? When we stop and reflect, when we give up the false dream and stick with it, the real dream emerges."

The Entrepreneurial Myth insists entrepreneurs take the *leap* of faith, *battle* competitors and *shake* things up; they're to fail *fast*, move *fast* and break things. They *run* businesses from business *accelerators*. Throughout the 30-year media sample underpinning this book, the image of the entrepreneur is always as proactive pursuer, aggressor and hunter, never the object of action.[196] Never the farmer. You are perhaps so used to seeing the entrepreneur fizzing with agency, energy and action, the title 'reflective entrepreneur' seems an oxymoron. There is something suspicious about a quietly contemplative entrepreneur, something of the night. A small business with limited growth is classed a lifestyle business, somehow not the real deal. Real entrepreneurship is supposed to be big and brash, fast and furious. Hunters rule!

But remember the tortoise and hare? Hare's frenzied arrogance slows him down; tortoise's steady consistency wins the race. Aesop's fable taught childhood lessons of 'more haste, less speed'. Perhaps, it could be that way with business?

Take inspiration from the planners who planted avenues of chestnut trees in London's Royal Parks over 400 years ago; they visualized promenades for their great, great, great, great grandchildren to enjoy. They had faith that the land would be cared for and enjoyed by people they would never meet. They trusted strangers.

Take inspiration from Carlo Petrini and the activists who founded the Slow Food movement in the 1980s to defend regional traditions and gastronomic pleasure. Initially a protest against plans to open a fast-food restaurant at Rome's Spanish Steps, now a global movement stretching from China to India, the US to Italy. Petrini has travelled from being an activist to become one of the United Nations' Environment Programme Champions.

Note the word, *inspiration*. This book doesn't advocate the wheels of business grind to a halt. Far from it. Quick decisions are undoubtedly needed. You must move deftly to fill that gap in the market. Snap judgements work.[197]

The question to consider is: what if a more reflective, contemplative and careful approach refined business decision making and saved the business? What if this clarity slowed the churn of business creation and failure in a significant proportion of cases?

This is controversial. You have heard how a pure economic lens seeks to churn businesses quicker. But this 'fifth time lucky' equation doesn't include the significant transaction costs and personal costs of losing a business in an imperfect market. Entrepreneurial success currently rests on the wrong metrics, say Davidow and Williams:[198] "The world needs us to be more than just economic units taking cues from a handful of gurus ... Our personal journeys have intrinsic value ... There are no winners and no losers, just journeyers."

Slow down, stretch and think. Take time. Extending the reach of enterprise policy beyond the four- or five-year parliamentary or presidential term might help businesses. Remember US business leader Alampi from Chapter 14? A thoughtful, methodical approach to his business stages might help in the midst of scale-up change. Slowing the churn of business creation and failure by 10% might mitigate hidden heartache. And if entrepreneurship takes a breath, and if you step out from under the Myth's façade, who are you?

Find out. It takes courage to be who we are and avoid our reflection in others' eyes, says Brett. Think about *where* you really are – *who* you really are – in your business. Gently, compassionately, pinch the gap closed. Courage is needed to separate from the Myth and stand authentically apart from others, Brett continues. Say to the business guru: isn't that interesting, that idea worked for you, I wonder what my version looks like? Adapt the business guru's mantra to empower your practice rather than accepting its competitive jibe to run even faster.

Sometimes the adventure doesn't work out. Some must go there, to come back. Many interviewees for this book could name the brutal moment of business jeopardy or failure: Brett on the day his practice closed, Hunter in his garden as the oil price slid, and in Chapter 22 you'll meet Lora Fachie on the London 2012 trackside. Remember your brutal moment? Perhaps it's yet to come. Either way, like the brave and brilliant contributors to this book, seize your unique opportunity to change. Post-traumatic growth is the jargon; instead of being put back just as you were before your work wrestle or business loss, exploit the chance to learn and grow. Decide to do things very differently next time. Start again. This is the process at the heart of entrepreneurial resilience. Perhaps only then are businesses two, three, four and five possible.

So: reflect, be brave, learn the lesson, start again. Stepping out of the shadow of The Entrepreneurial Myth as you really are demands courage. Who is waiting for you? Where is your collective? And how will you reach them? Next, is the manifesto pledge to CONNECT.

CHAPTER 20.
CONNECT

HEROIC TEAMS

Colin O'Donnell is a serial technology entrepreneur focused on some of the biggest challenges facing our cities. He was a founding partner of the seminal digital/physical technology and design company, Control Group, acquired by a subsidiary of Google in 2015. His work is regularly featured in *TechCrunch*, *Fast Company*, *Wired* and *The New York Times*. "An entrepreneur might be someone who opens a dry cleaner, or someone running a Fortune 500 enterprise. It's unhelpful to lump them all together," explains O'Donnell, running between appointments. "I've experienced different styles of entrepreneurship loosely related to the capital that backs them. Start-up entrepreneurs backed by venture capital are incredibly risk tolerant. They seek 10x solutions and 10x returns – in other words, the vision and drive to make something ten times better, not 10%, and return ten times the investment. So, if 80% to 90% fail, it's tolerated. These entrepreneurs move fast, take chances and work long hours with a small team

– I'm trying not to use the word – but it is aggressive. Then there is the CEO who is backed by private equity looking for 20% returns; they are operationally driven and want consistent leadership to grow their success.

"It's important the right entrepreneur is focused on the right problem. If somebody is naturally more comfortable with risk, they'll be less excited about implementing scaleable business processes; if somebody needs stability, they'll be better equipped to deliver second stage growth. We categorize different types of people and try to make everyone the same. I often hear: 'can't we all be 10x thinkers?' But the fact is we need the majority to produce steady returns, so the outliers can focus on doing something completely different. Exchange the two and you'll end up with disastrous results.

"It's like the baseball strategy of consistently hitting line drives, versus swinging for home runs. We applaud the home run because it's easier to see Babe Ruth. But if he wasn't supported by his team who consistently bring in the wins, it wouldn't work. Just focusing on the few interesting people who have broken the mould obscures the massive business machine behind them. There is an untold story of amazing operators focused on making sure their business is successful."

Ex-ad man Mark Earls[199] revealed how Western individualism has produced the stubborn belief that some individuals are better, cleverer and more knowledgeable than others.[200] There is only one Babe Ruth. In this cultural frame, The Entrepreneurial Myth presents a lone wolf focused on solitary glory.

But real business is delivered by teams. Do you have one? Among entrepreneurs, 84% start their businesses with other people.[201] Ancient stories and myths ensure every hero has an alter ego to provide missing qualities and characteristics. The hero's buddy makes him 'whole'.

Collective entrepreneurship – a term used to describe the group of co-founders, advisors and helpers that sustain new entrepreneurial businesses – [202] benefits from diverse views and skills, a range of financial and human capital.[203] Venture capitalists ascribe more importance to the capabilities of the team, rather than a talented individual. There is some evidence that team ventures edge ahead in revenue and performance.[204] The notion that collective intelligence can produce better results than individuals rings true time and time again.[205]

The entrepreneur is categorically not alone but remains lonely.[206] There is a psychological – not physical – distance between an entrepreneur and those they work with. This is the space in which the Myth plays. The good news is you can reach across this gap.

Robert Reich, who served three US administrations, urged readers of the *Harvard Business Review* to recognize and reward the team as the hero.[207] The American Dream is built on "the familiar tale of triumphant individuals, of enterprising heroes who win riches and rewards through a combination of Dale Carnegie-esque self-improvement, Norman Vincent Peale-esque faith, Sylvester Stallone-esque assertiveness and plain old-fashioned good luck." Yet refusing to acknowledge the presence and talent of the hero entrepreneur's team stymies economic success. "We need to honour our teams more, our aggressive leaders and maverick geniuses less," he argued. If you want to see vivid examples of collective entrepreneurship, don't look in your newspaper's business section, he says. Look to the sports pages. Teams win. This is a long game.

Reich called for a collective entrepreneurship in the 1980s. Ten years later, the concept of post-heroic leadership[208] surfaced, advocating businesses driven through consensus with co-workers, not the unitary command of a "great man". Scholars admit post-heroic business remains "mostly invisible"[209] outside academic journals. Another ten years and the word 'collective' still clashes with the free-market economic principles that underscore the word 'entrepreneurship'. "As a society, we are wary of the old Cs associated with sharing: cooperatives, collectives and communal structures," says Ted Talk star Rachel Botsman.[210] "The words themselves are loaded with stigma ... Perhaps we fear they will jeopardize our cherished personal freedoms of individuality, privacy and autonomy."

These personal freedoms may well be illusory if an essential supporting cast of team and state is hidden. Mariana Mazzucato[211] argues that the state acts as an entrepreneurial agent investing money and embracing risk to create the right conditions for innovation – a role often underplayed and misunderstood. The lone entrepreneur couldn't succeed in technological innovation, clean tech or green energy, she argues, without the state's preparatory intervention. Much lies beneath and beyond individual entrepreneurial genius.

There is an educational skew to the lone individualist too. As O'Donnell noted when interviewed for this book, business schools *equip* people to be excellent operators, but graduate *ambition* is disproportionately dominated by the 10x thinkers. The majority hanker to disrupt industry, yet it is essential the majority maintain and curate industry. This is the creativity myth.[212] "We are addicted to game-changing," explains Michael Bhaskar in his book *Curation*, "and the idea that creation and creativity are intrinsic goods." While society needs the disruptive, game-changing 10x thinkers – the stereotypical entrepreneur of the Myth – it also needs people who refine, simplify, explain and support. Society needs *curators* as well as creators; *operators* as well as entrepreneurs; *farmers* as well as hunters. And entrepreneurship needs well-balanced teams and communities.

There is a deep irony that while numerous entrepreneurial businesses successfully harness the power of community in their products and services – think of Uber, Airbnb, WeWork and eBay – the same powerful processes aren't applied to entrepreneurship itself. Imagine if it was different. Imagine if the solo entrepreneurial hero was banished once and for all. What would happen if the principles of collaborative culture – the same principles behind the phenomenal success of so many businesses – were applied to entrepreneurial talent? It's time to change.

Entrepreneurship is a broad and complex church; refuse the narrow, noisy metrics for the 10x thinker (unless you know you are one of them). Curators, operators and farmers are driven by a different – but essential – purpose. When the world offers you more roles and relationships, connections and opportunities, data and decisions than you need, the quality of your choice is paramount. "In an overloaded world, the locus of value is shifting. Tech companies have known this for a while. From their position on the frontline of overload, they realized that taking away, curating, is important ... Curation strategies work against the trend towards overload. Curation helps cut through overload and navigate this new economic phase"[213] Focus on the wrong definition of success, for you, and you are more likely to fail.

Seek feedback. Decide: are you a raw creator or refined curator? Or something else altogether? "The leaders I've encountered are highly receptive to giving feedback, making connections, linking potential partners, customers and investors together," adds O'Donnell. "If the smart people in an industry pull in the same direction, it benefits us all. Ask." Adopt the role that fits, not a clichéd entrepreneurial stereotype. Reach out to the team already around you. Build a new one. Let people in. It's time to belong. Hold on tight to the evidence that collective intelligence and teamwork trumps individualism. Gut The Entrepreneurial Myth and turn it inside out. Real business wisdom lies in a community of talents around you. Now, use it.

So, discover your purpose, find your collective, share talents and teams. It's time to think differently. Next is the manifesto pledge to LEARN.

CHAPTER 21.
LEARN

THINK ABOUT BUSINESS FAILURE LIKE AN AVIATOR

Gretchen Haskins is CEO of HeliOffshore, a company dedicated to global offshore helicopter safety. Gretchen has served on the board of the UK Civil Aviation Authority, the board of National Air Traffic Services (NATS), in the US Air Force and as an expert advisor to NATO on human performance. "In the aviation industry, we have become students of our own performance," asserts Haskins brightly. "We're inspired by those brave, pioneering aviators who took to the skies as their own test pilots. I was told a fascinating story by the son of one of aviation's founding fathers; his father had been in the room when there was an early discussion about the possibility of pre-flight checklists to standardise take-off procedures throughout the industry. Most saw it as an unnecessary bureaucracy and burden. But one person in the room thought about it and said: good idea, I'm going to try it. This was the beginning of real understanding and sharing and learning. It was the beginning of accident investigation, pooling expertise and adapting flight procedures accordingly. It ultimately propelled aviation much further than those brilliant pioneers could even imagine at the time.

"This is powerful for me because my mother fell asleep at the wheel of the car she was driving. She wasn't wearing a seat belt and died instantly. Now imagine if, as you fell asleep at the wheel, you could detect it and recover before you hit something. Imagine if you did hit something, you survived.

"Thousands of people die daily in car accidents. Yet the data proves it is possible to design out risk. Innovations like airbags, blind spot mirrors, driver's licences, minimum drinking age legislation, have saved lives. The opportunity is there to create and implement a coherent strategy to save more lives earlier. Policy works best this way: ask the questions, consider what good looks like, create the solution, then drive the collective effort to ensure the good stuff happens across the world sooner.

"You can design out failure. In 1997, aviation industry leaders gathered to debate the 200 accidents that had occurred over the previous decade. They said: if we keep going, our industry is over, people won't fly, we must intervene. They formed the Commercial Aviation Safety Team (CAST) as an integrated, data-driven response to reduce commercial aviation fatalities. The dark days following 9/11 meant airlines were going bankrupt yet CAST stuck to the goal to reduce fatalities by 80%. They set their mind to examine each failure, create strategy to address the main causes for that failure and inspire collaborative action between regulators, airlines, manufacturers, pilots and engineers. It took ten years, but they did it. They reduced fatalities by 80% and saved millions at the same time.

"Understand failure; then collaborate to address it. It works. This demands a 'just' culture so all understand we're going to learn from failure, not measure each other against it.

"Initially, aviation safety focused on the equipment. Mend the machine and you're safe. But when you've solved the mechanical problem, you reveal human failure. You reveal organizational failure. If one person makes an error, it's down to that individual. If several people make the same mistake, it's a system problem. Working conditions need attention perhaps, or the data available to inform decisions; maybe it's the tools people have to do their job, or how people are trained. Considering the whole team as a system elevates success beyond the nuts and bolts of the aircraft. When considering the success and safety of complex systems – like flights, like businesses – only this holistic perspective drives the breakthroughs we need. The last thing US Airways Captain Chesley Sullenberger asked his co-pilot before he landed his plane on the Hudson was 'do you have any other ideas?' Sully personified a trait Lufthansa's Robert Schröder calls confident humility. To err is human, of course. But it is how you identify and recover and learn from these challenges that is important. It is your ability to analyse the system, understand yourself, turn to the team.

"You get even better results if you call failure 'performance'. The safety industry has gained much ground with the argument, 'hey, you don't want to be the one who kills someone!' But I'm amazed by how much more traction you gain saying, 'don't you want to be excellent where it really counts?' If you turn tackling failure into improving performance, into the continuous pursuit of excellence, you swap an accusation for an opportunity. We must ultimately move from studying failure to studying performance.

"So, analyse what it will it take to achieve your aim. Resolve to build the necessary trust between the people who have a crucial part to play. Decide how you will inspire them to work together to share data and strategy, to design out failure and craft the future. Then you'll see the results the aviation industry has achieved over the past 50 years, but faster. Much faster."

Entrepreneurship is currently in the equivalent of the first days of flight. Look how high the superstar flies! How brave! Follow the aviation industry's timeline; now imagine you are the person in the room advocating pre-flight checklists for business. Imagine you investigated and analysed business failure with a cool head, instead of a shamed heart.

The aptly named Professor James Reason created his 'Swiss cheese model'[214] as a way of envisioning how 'holes' in an organization's defensive layers align to create the perfect conditions for failure. His acclaimed model is used widely in engineering and aviation sectors; more recently in medical and healthcare settings. What if this rigor was applied to the failure of entrepreneurial businesses?

A business is a complex system seething with multiple fallible decisions, interpersonal dynamics and uncontrollable external influences. A business 'hole' might be a duff management decision impacting cash flow or prolonged absence of one of your operational team; it might be a change in your customer or supplier's strategy, a new business rates regime or wider economic recession. Your business is probably resilient and flexible enough to survive one, even two, of these 'holes'. But if all the 'holes' aligned, would your business fold?

"Errors and violations are commonplace, banal even," says Reason. "They are as much part of the human condition as breathing, eating, sleeping and dying ... [It is a] widespread myth that errors occur 'out of the blue' and are highly variable in their form. Neither is the case. Errors are not random and they take recurrent and predictable forms."[215]

This means you could analyse situational, geographical, task-related and time-related clusters of failed entrepreneurial businesses. This would demand both individual and collective mindfulness.[216] It would demand an alert, inquisitive striving for a more reflective, more effective entrepreneurship. It requires an open national business culture where entrepreneurs share and report failure factors without fear of shame, blame and recourse. It rests on Schröder's confident humility.

Entrepreneurial shame cripples lives, communities and economies as it limits the honest exchange of learning, advice and support. "Shame is very clever because it whispers in your ear: 'you must never speak the truth, I'm your friend, let me protect you,'" says Brett. "But shame only exists in silence; the moment you speak up, it cannot exist." Are you ready to speak up? Let's pool the data of the 90%, draw the patterns and learn the lessons.

Of course, personal qualities still matter; business creation will always have room for great leadership, professionalism, skill, improvisation and luck. James Reason proposed that the human contribution to the performance of any system could be heroic as well as hazardous.[217] But let's change a system that is helplessly skewed to blame and shame individual entrepreneurs for business failure without essential collective analysis of why the majority of entrepreneurial businesses flounder. Let's change a system that encourages more and more entrepreneurs to shoulder personal risk, to keep the enterprise funnel healthy, without the wisdom and learning from the wasted 90%. If aviation, energy, banking and healthcare can learn from Reason, so can entrepreneurship.

Blaming individuals may be emotionally satisfying and culturally convenient, but consider the prize if systems analysis improved the business success rate by just 10%. Quick calculations sketch the potential of £19.6 billion to the UK economy and $850 billion to the US economy, plus the unquantifiable human benefit of preserving entrepreneurial well-being.

Let's follow Haskins and become students of our own performance. Be the person in the room ready to try. Let's set an audacious goal. Is a 10% improvement in the business success rate enough? What about 20%? Or 80%? Pick a number. Imagine a business environment where no business failed for lack of financial expertise or legal understanding, or for pride, or fear, or ego. Gather data, share data, analyse data. Gather together to strip The Entrepreneurial Myth of its authority by designing out business failure and designing in business success.

There is a real business revolution brewing. There is work to do. But it is a marathon, not a sprint. Next, is the manifesto pledge to PERSIST.

CHAPTER 22.
PERSIST

THINK ABOUT BUSINESS SUCCESS LIKE AN ATHLETE

Lora Fachie is a Paralympian cyclist who holds 11 world championship medals, a bronze and gold medal from the Rio 2016 Paralympic Games and the Paralympic record in the tandem pursuit race. In 2019, Lora launched her own lifestyle and nutrition consultancy business with her husband and fellow Paralympian Neil Fachie. She hopes to defend her title in the Tokyo 2020 Paralympic Games. "I was suddenly, painfully, deposited in a heap on the road," Fachie admits, wincing. "My bike was broken, I lost a lot of skin, my tandem partner had broken her collarbone. I had felt invincible at the beginning of the race. Other people crash their bikes, I thought. Not me. It was a shocking introduction to the danger of my sport. It took time to rebuild my confidence and race with bikes around me.

"But London 2012 was on the horizon and this was the event that had inspired me to get on my bike in the first place. I picked myself up because I desperately wanted to be a Paralympic champion on home turf. I wanted to be part of it. Leading up to the London 2012, I enjoyed several strong races so was hopeful for a medal. I had four events and four chances.

"The Games arrived. I finished fourth in my first two events. The worst place. All that hard work but absolutely nothing to show for it. Next, I had two road events. We call the road time trial the 'race of truth' because there is nowhere to hide. In other races, you can be clever and sit in the wheels, get pulled around, then outsprint everyone at the finish. The smartest, not the strongest, person wins. I love that you have to be the strongest to win a time trial.

"My partner and I were leading, we were 15 seconds up, we only had five kilometres to go! I was aware we were winning because of the roar of the crowd!

"But we turned the corner and our bike chain jammed. We came to a standstill. We had to get off the bike. That was my gold medal, gone. It was the lowest point of my career. After we crossed the line seventh, I just sat beside the track and cried. I decided I would never put myself in that position again; I would never get on a bike again. I had failed my family. Only now, I can see how narrow-minded it was to think it was the end of the world. But that was the moment, that was rock bottom.

"I changed my mind and changed my mentality. I thought I would try just one more year. I had to learn how to enjoy the process of getting to my goal, to make my goal worth it. There are so many successful sportspeople I look up to who haven't won their gold medal but still stand as phenomenal athletes in their own right. Usually, my riding is constantly observed and analysed: my heart rate, the power I push through the peddle, how each muscle fires, is carefully considered. I stripped things back. Now I occasionally step back and say, 'no data or analysis today, no feedback, just the ride'. This perspective matters.

"I asked for help to see things differently. We aren't born skilled, we need help. When you get to the start line, there is a massive expert team behind you: two coaches, two physiotherapists, nutritionist, physiologist. One person has a medal round their neck, but you don't stand there alone.

"Incredibly, 12 months on from London 2012, I was world champion in the event that had floored me. Gold in Rio 2016 followed. It was a shock to win my medal in the velodrome pursuit, but I took my medal and I won't give it back! My failures make my story. Success has been so much sweeter following the disappointment.

"In any form of living – business, family, sport – you will have hiccups and hurdles. But what will you learn along the way? Ask yourself, 'am I doing what I need to do to be happy?' If so, keep going. If not, do something, change something. I changed my approach: if I don't win this medal, I'm still me, I'm no different. Winning won't make you happy, it doesn't change you as a person. Ironically, if you are happy first, you will be more likely to be successful. A happy rider is a fast rider. I only discovered this when I got off my bike."

No revolution is easy. It might take four years, eight years, 12 years. Listen to Fachie: there is as much work to do off the bike, as on it. Are you up to it?

'Resilience' risks becoming a buzzword fizzing through corporate culture without settling. At first glance, it is a defensive construct to bolster the status quo. Don't tackle the societal or cultural reasons for our 'harder, better, faster' work cultures or, indeed, deal with the demands of The Entrepreneurial Myth. Instead, bolster those under pressure; sell a personal solution to mitigate an institutional pressure. But real resilience is much more than bouncing back or papering over the cracks.

Resilience first became the subject of academic research in the 1970s and a handful of studies[218] have tracked the link between the concept and entrepreneurial business success. While more research is needed, the concept of resilience borrows from theories of post-traumatic growth – remember Brett in Chapter 19? Instead of demanding a stiff upper lip and Pollyanna smile, resilience is really about becoming stronger or more resourceful as a result of an experience. Reivich and Shatte[219] defined learnable skills of resilience: self-awareness and confidence in own abilities, impulse control and the capacity to analyse the big picture, empathy and the ability to connect with others, optimism and a willingness to experience new situations to grow.

Resilience is one of four psychological states propping up your psychological capital.[220] You need high levels of psychological capital to improve any area of life. According to an academic called Luthans,[221] four things combine for optimum performance: start with *self-efficacy* or belief in your own ability, add *hope* or the ability to persevere, now add *optimism* and *resilience*. You will not only perform, but bloom. Just like Fachie.

This book started with hope. All entrepreneurs share the creation of opportunity, opportunity sparks hope, and you chase hope wherever it leads. Here is the opportunity to reshape a reflective, resilient entrepreneurship for the next generation.

Listen. There isn't a secret formula; there isn't a magic sauce. Pay no attention to the man behind the curtain. Luthans' psychological states are moods and habits. Consider your talents and abilities afresh. Learn to assume the best; study and analyse ambiguity; persevere nevertheless. Reject The Entrepreneurial Myth's lies that you must be special and invincible and alone. Instead, bank psychological capital. Just as Haskin recommended, stop black and white thinking about success and failure. Instead, become a student of your own performance in a diverse community of talents. Your Real Business Revolution starts today.

What are you waiting for?

FUTURE
ENTREPRENEUR

The Myth excludes talent, isolates business creators and jeopardizes entrepreneurial mental health; it justifies appalling business failure rates and skews enterprise policy.

It is time to change. Education and policy must pivot to meet real business priorities. Adoring mythmaking must be tempered with real stories about real business. And the gap between entrepreneurial idolatry and real business must be pinched closed.

Welcome to the real business manifesto.

This is an opportunity to SPEAK up, be frank, listen hard and be well. Take off the entrepreneurial mask. Learn a new business vocabulary that includes 'but', 'not too good' and 'help'. Hold up your colleague's mirror, as they hold up yours. Co-create an entrepreneurship wide enough and broad enough for failure.

This is an opportunity to REFLECT, be brave, have the courage to be imperfect. Be the tortoise, be the journeyer. Think. Take time. Seek clarity to slow business churn. Share your brutal moment, learn the lesson, start all over again.

This is an opportunity to CONNECT with your collective – perhaps a handful of 10x thinkers, perhaps a global community of curators, operators and farmers. Claim your purpose. Name the team as hero.

This is an opportunity to LEARN as we think about failure like an aviator. Become a student of your own performance. Adopt Schröder's confident humility; adapt Reason's 'Swiss cheese model'. Design out failure by studying performance.

And in all these things, PERSIST as we think about business success like an athlete. Know that the best sit at the trackside sometimes. Study the learnable skills of resilience. Bank psychological capital. Understand there is as much work to do off the bike as on it. But the prize is open to a diverse community of talents – a community that welcomes you and celebrates you.

Entrepreneurship has a real future. This book rests on analysis of a 30-year media sample and tour of 50 years of enterprise policy initiatives. Entrepreneurship is as glittering and intoxicating as ever. Can you see it clearly now?

There is a billion-dollar prize if you challenge, analyse and work to change appalling business failure rates. There is a priceless opportunity to ease entrepreneurial mental health challenges and boost business well-being. There is an opportunity to coach each other and encourage each other so entrepreneurship is a more reflective, resilient and effective force for good.

You are invited to speak, reflect, connect, learn and persist in a movement to preserve the best of real entrepreneurial business.

Are you in?

ENDNOTES

1. The Start Up Low Down, How Start Ups Are Changing Britain
    - Virgin Start Up report, Published November 2016 by Virgin
    in partnership with the Centre for Economics and Business
    Research. This concluded that start-ups contribute £196 billion
    (as Gross Value Added) to the UK economy. This is the equivalent
    of approximately 10% of GDP.

2. The US small business community contributes approximately
    half of the country's total $17 trillion GDP. Statistic sourced
    from data gathered 2017. See https://townsquared.com/ts/
    resources/small-business-united-states-numbers/ for data on
    the contribution of small and entrepreneurial businesses to the
    US economy. See also https://www.sba.gov/sites/default/files/
    advocacy/Frequently-Asked-Questions-Small-Business-2018.pdf

3. Nicolson, L. (2001) 'Modelling The Evolution Of Entrepreneurial
    Mythology'. MSc Entrepreneurship. University of Aberdeen.
    September 2001 (unpublished).

4. Gartner, William B., "'Who is an Entrepreneur?' is the Wrong
    Question" University of Illinois at Urbana-Champaign's Academy
    for Entrepreneurial Leadership Historical Research Reference in
    Entrepreneurship (1988).

5. See Linda Yueh, *The Great Economists. How Their Ideas Can Help Us Today* (London: Viking an imprint of Penguin Books, 2018) 159.

6. Businessman and author Warren Blanks.

7. Nicolson, L. (2001) 'Modelling The Evolution Of Entrepreneurial Mythology'.

8. Nicholson, Louise, and Alistair R. Anderson. "News and Nuances of the Entrepreneurial Myth and Metaphor: Linguistic Games in Entrepreneurial Sense–Making and Sense–Giving." *Entrepreneurship Theory and Practice* 29, no. 2 (March 2005): 153–72.

9. See research by Dr. Michael A Freeman, University of California San Francisco, http://www.michaelafreemanmd.com/Research.html In particular, his pre-publication manuscript *Are Entrepreneurs 'Touched with Fire'?* (17 April 2015).

10. See Mariana Mazzucato, *The Entrepreneurial State. Debunking Public versus Private Sector Myths* (London: Penguin Random House UK, 2018) 4, 26, 52. "Small business associations have convinced governments in many countries that they are underfunded as a category. Yet in many countries, they receive more support than the police force (!), without providing the jobs or innovation that help justify such support ... Hughes (2008) has shown that in the UK, SMEs received close to £9 billion in direct and indirect government support, which is more than the police force receives".

11. For example, see Office of National Statistics Statistical Bulletin, *Business Demography UK*, published November 2017, which shows the business birth rate increased, along with the business death rate, between 2011 and 2016.

12. Kishore Mahbubani, *The Great Convergence. Asia, the West and the Logic of One World* (New York: Public Affairs, 2013) 195.

13. See www.scientificamerican.com/article/women-talk-more-than-men/

14. Vesey and Foulkes, *Collins Dictionary of Philosophy* (Glasgow: HarperCollins, 1990).

15. Heartfelt thanks to Colin Brett for this term.

16. Gergen. K, Constructionist Dialogues and the Vicissitudes of the Political, cited in Ed. Velody, *The Politics of Social Construction* (London: Sage, 1998).

17. See Hodge and Kress, *Social Semiotics* (Cambridge: Polity Press, 1988).

18. Hall. S, 1980, *Encoding/decoding in Culture, Media, Language. Working Papers in Cultural Studies 1972-79,* University of Birmingham, Hutchinson & Co., London.

19. Walter R. Fisher, *Human Communication as Narration: Toward a Philosophy of Reason, Value and Action* (Columbia: University of South Carolina Press, 1987), 138.

20. Frosh. S, *Psychoanalysis and Psychology: Minding the Gap* (London: Macmillan, 1989).

21. Statistic generated in 2017 by www.radicati.com

22. Bernstein cited in Allan. S, *News Culture* (Buckingham: Open University Press, 1999) 185.

23. Evan Davis, *Post-truth. Peak Bullshit And What We Can Do About It* (London: Abacus, 2018) xxvi.

24. See research by Dr Michael A Freeman, University of California San Francisco, http://www.michaelafreemanmd.com/Research.html. In particular, his pre-publication manuscript *Are Entrepreneurs 'Touched with Fire'?* (17 April 2015).

25. Swart, Chisholm and Brown, *Neuroscience for Leadership* (Basingstoke, Hampshire: Palgrave Macmillan, 2015).

26. See Mark Earls, *Herd. How to Change Mass Behaviour By Harnessing Our True Nature* (Chichester, West Sussex: John Wiley & Sons, 2009).

27. See Christopher Booker, *The Seven Basic Plots. Why We Tell Stories* (London: Continuum, 2004) 6. Followed by Joseph Campbell, *The Hero with a Thousand Faces* (Novato, CA: New World Library, 2008).

28. Richard Branson, *Finding My Virginity* (London: Penguin Random House, 2017) 344, 353.

29. Yan Qicheng, *Jack Ma and Alibaba: A business and life biography* (London: LID Publishing Ltd, 2017) 46.

30. Valentina Zayra, "Female founders got 2% of Venture Capital Dollars in 2017", *Forbes*, published 31 January 2018.

31. Anne McPherson, "Female Business Owners – What the Banks Should do to Help", *The Guardian*, published 10 April 2013.

32. McKinsey cited in Rand Fishkin, *Lost and Founder. A Painfully Honest Field Guide to the Startup World* (London: Penguin Random House UK, 2018) 157.

33. Nicolson, L. (2001) 'Modelling The Evolution Of Entrepreneurial Mythology'.

34. Helena Morrissey, *A Good Time to be a Girl: Don't Lean In, Change The System* (London: William Collins, An Imprint of Harper Collins Publishers, 2018). This is essential reading; I buy this book for every woman I mentor.

35. The UK Centre for Entrepreneurs recently studied how gender influences entrepreneurship.

36. Valnetina Zayra, "Female founders got 2% of Venture Capital Dollars in 2017", *Forbes*, published 31 January 2018.

37. Both Branson and Musk cited in Shelley Davidow and Paul Williams, *Fail Brilliantly. Exploding the Myths of failure and Success* (USA: Familius Books, 2017) 68.

38. Myrto Pantazi, Mikhail Kissine, and Olivier Klein (2018). The Power of the Truth Bias: False Information Affects Memory and Judgment Even in the Absence of Distraction. *Social Cognition*: Vol. 36, No. 2, pp. 167-198.

39. Shelley Davidow and Paul Williams, *Fail Brilliantly. Exploding the Myths of failure and Success* (USA: Familius Books, 2017) 38.

40. Jeffrey Pfeffer, "Barriers to the Advance of Organisational Science: Paradigm Development as a Dependent Variable," *The Academy of Management Review*, Vol.18 No.4 (October 1993), p599-620.

41. Shelley Davidow and Paul Williams, *Fail Brilliantly. Exploding the Myths of failure and Success* (USA: Familius Books, 2017), 72.

42. Shelley Davidow and Paul Williams, *Fail Brilliantly. Exploding the Myths of failure and Success* (USA: Familius Books, 2017), 15.

43. Bob Keiller was Chairman of Scottish Enterprise between 2016 and 2018. Throughout his career, he has been declared Entrepreneur of the Year, twice, Grampian Industrialist of the Year, and Scottish Businessman of the Year. Bob was awarded a CBE in the 2017 Queen's Birthday Honours list for services to business and entrepreneurship. He was interviewed for this book in November 2018.

44. Cited in Kishore Mahbubani, *The Great Convergence. Asia, the West and the Logic of One World* (New York: Public Affairs, 2013) 33.

45. See Mark Earls, *Herd. How to Change Mass Behaviour By Harnessing Our True Nature* (Chichester, West Sussex: John Wiley & Sons, 2009) 109.

46. Hill and Levenhagen, 1995, Metaphors and Mental Models: Sensemaking and Sensegiving in Innovative and Entrepreneurial Activities. *Journal of Management* Vol.21, No.6, p1057.

47. Choi. Y. B., *Paradigms and Conventions: Uncertainty, Decisionmaking and Entrepreneurship* (Michigan: University of Michigan Press, 1993).

48. Lakoff and Johnson, *Metaphors We Live By* (Chicago: University of Chicago Press, 1980).

49. Koiranen, 1995, North European Metaphors of 'Entrepreneurship' and 'an Entrepreneur', *Frontiers of Entrepreneurship Research 1995*, Ed. Bygrave et al, P&R Publications, Waltham MA.

50. Lissack. M, 1997, Knowledge is not Infrastructure: applying metaphorical lessons from complexity science. Presented to the London School of Economics Seminar Series on Complexity, February 1997.

51. Stephen, Ute, Entrepreneurs' mental health and well-being: a review and research agenda, *Academy of Management Perspectives* 2018 Vol.32 No.3 290-322.

52. For insight into urban isolation see Olivia Laing, *The Lonely City. Adventures In The Art Of Being Alone* (Edinburgh: Canongate Books, 2017).

53. Remember Kate Spade, Ilya Zhitomirskly, Jody Sherman, Aaron Swartz, Austen Heinz and Faigy Mayer.

54. See research by Dr Michael A Freeman, University of California San Francisco, http://www.michaelafreemanmd.com/ Research.html. In particular, his pre-publication manuscript *Are Entrepreneurs 'Touched with Fire'?* (17 April 2015).

55. Study by Dr Michael Freeman, clinical professor at University of California, San Francisco.

56. Rand Fishkin, *Lost and Founder: A Painfully Honest Field Guide To The Startup World* (London: Penguin Random House UK, 2018).

57. For example, Preventing Start-up Suicide, Literally by John Arnold in *Entrepreneur* magazine; or The Psychological Price of Entrepreneurship by Jessica Bruder in *Inc* Magazine. See blogs by Brad Feld, Sean Percival and Mark Suster.

58. Gartner, William B., "'Who Is an Entrepreneur?' Is the Wrong Question" University of Illinois at Urbana-Champaign's Academy for Entrepreneurial Leadership Historical Research Reference in Entrepreneurship (1988).

59. Walter Isaacson, *Steve Jobs* (London: Abacus, 2015) 109.

60. Yan Qicheng, *Jack Ma and Alibaba: A business and life biography* (London: LID Publishing Ltd, 2017) 59.

61. Ashlee Vance, *Elon Musk* (London: Virgin Books, 2016).

62. Ashlee Vance, *Elon Musk* (London: Virgin Books, 2016) 24.

63. Ashlee Vance, *Elon Musk* (London: Virgin Books, 2016) 344.

64. Ashlee Vance, *Elon Musk* (London: Virgin Books, 2016) 361

65. Ashlee Vance, *Elon Musk* (London: Virgin Books, 2016) 22.

66. See research led by Swinburne University of Technology in Melbourne, Australia, cited in popular business blogs.

67. Or the American Psychiatric Association's Diagnostic and Statistical Manual of Mental Disorders.

68. For example, see Stephen, Ute, Entrepreneurs' mental health and well-being: a review and research agenda, Academy of Management Perspectives 2018 Vol.32 No.3 290-322.

69. See Michael A Freeman "Are Entrepreneurs 'Touched with Fire'?" Pre-publication manuscript available on http://www. michaelafreemanmd.com/Research.html University of California San Francisco, 6.

70. Stephen, Ute, Entrepreneurs' mental health and well-being: a review and research agenda, *Academy of Management Perspectives* 2018 Vol.32 No.3 290-322.

71. Stephen, Ute, Entrepreneurs' mental health and well-being: a review and research agenda, *Academy of Management Perspectives* 2018 Vol.32 No.3 290-322.

72. Study by Dr Michael Freeman, clinical professor at University of California, San Francisco.

73. John Gartner cited in The Psychological Price of Entrepreneurship by Jessica Bruder in *Inc* magazine.

74. Lihui Yang and Deming An, with Jessica Anderson Turner, *Handbook of Chinese Mythology* (New York: Oxford University Press, 2005) 46.

75. Lihui Yang and Deming An, with Jessica Anderson Turner, *Handbook of Chinese Mythology* (New York: Oxford University Press, 2005) 57.

76. William Radice, *Myths and Legends of India* (London: The Folio Society, 2001) 613 – 614.

77. See Christopher Booker, *The Seven Basic Plots. Why We Tell Stories* (London: Continuum, 2004) 347, 425, 488.

78. See Linda Yueh, *The Great Economists. How Their Ideas Can Help Us Today* (London: Viking an imprint of Penguin Books, 2018) 25.

79. See Linda Yueh, *The Great Economists. How Their Ideas Can Help Us Today* (London: Viking an imprint of Penguin Books, 2018) 159.

80. David Cameron Party Conference Speech, March 2011.

81. 'Build it in Britain' speech at the EEF Technology Hub on Tuesday 24th July 2018. Source Larbour.org.uk.

82. 'Build it in Britain' speech at the EEF Technology Hub on Tuesday 24th July 2018. Source Larbour.org.uk.

83. See The Federation of Small Businesses discussion paper 'Enterprise 2050 Getting UK Enterprise Policy Right' February 2013. It concluded: "Overall, what emerges from this review of both current and previous enterprise policies is a 'patchwork quilt', 'chaos', 'labyrinth of initiatives' or 'muddle' (Audit Commission 1999, DTI/HM Treasury 2002, DTI, 2007) of government initiatives to support small businesses."

84. David Birch, The Job Generation Process (Cambridge, M.I.T Program on Neighbourhood and Regional Change, 1979).

85. Margaret Thatcher was Prime Minister between 1979 and 1990.

86. Thatcher, Margaret. "Speech to Small Business Bureau Conference" (speech, Surrey, February 8, 1984), Margaret Thatcher Foundation.

87. Thatcher, Margaret. "Speech to Small Business Bureau Conference" (speech, Surrey, February 8, 1984), Margaret Thatcher Foundation.

88. Francis Greene, "An Investigation into Enterprise Support For Younger People, 1975-2000," *International Small Business Journal: Researching Entrepreneurship* Volume 20 Issue 3 (August 2002): 315-336.

89. There were 103 initiatives introduced between 1982 and 1989 in comparison with 33 initiatives from 1971 to 1981.

90. Jonathan Guthrie, "Entrepreneur was key to reforms in 1980s." *Financial Times*, November 19, 2010.

91. Thatcher, Margaret. "Speech for BIC Enterprise Day" (speech, East London, June 19, 1989), Margaret Thatcher Foundation.

92. Francis Greene. 2002. 'An Investigation into Enterprise Support For Younger People, 1975-2000, *International Small Business Journal*. 20, no 3: 315-336.

93. Ronald Reagan was President of the United States of America between 1981 and 1989.

94. As stated by Thatcher's long-serving press secretary, Sir Bernard Ingham in a 2013 CNN interview.

95. Birch, David G.W., The Job Generation Process (1979). MIT Program on Neighborhood and Regional Change, Vol. , 302 pp 1979.

96. Reagan, Ronald. "Radio Address to the Nation on Small Business,"May 14, 1983. Online by Gerhard Peters and John T. Woolley, The American Presidency Project.

97. The Small Business Economic Policy Act 1980; The Small Business Innovation Research Programme 1982; The Prompt Payments Act; The Federal Technology Transfer Act 1986.

98. Ronald Reagan, Address to the Nation on Tax Reform, 29 May 1985.

99. George H. W. Bush was President of the United States of America between 1989 and 1993.

100. Bill Clinton (Democrat) was President of the US between 1992 and 2001.

101. The Taxpayer Relief Act 1997 and the Kennedy-Kassebaum Health Insurance Portability and Accountability Act (HIPAA) enacted in 1996.

102. See Greene, Francis and Patel, Priyen. *Enterprise 2050: Getting UK Enterprise Policy right"* (London: Federation of Small Business, 2013) 21-22.

103. See Francis Greene's 'An Investigation into Enterprise Support for Younger People, 1975-2000'.

104. John Major (Conservative) was the UK Prime Minister between 1990 and 1997.

105. Robert Gavron, Marc Cowling, Gerald Holtham and Andrea Westall, *The Entrepreneurial Society* (London, IPPR, 2000).

106. Robert Wapshott, "Small and medium-sized enterprise policy: Designed to fail?," *Environment and Planning C: Politics and Space* (2017): 750-772.

107. Tony Blair (Labour) was the UK Prime Minister between 1997 and 2007.

108. Quote from a speech made by Tony Blair in 1999 when he announced a £50m fund to stimulate further venture capital funding for start-up businesses.

109. Quote from a speech made by Tony Blair in 1999 at the Chicago Economic Club.

110. British Chambers of Commerce research cited in Madeleine Acey, "Small Business Service Scrapped" *The Times*, 26 October 2006.

111. Francis Greene and Priyen Patel, *Enterprise 2050: Getting UK enterprise policy right* (London: Federation of Small Businesses, 2013), *11-12*.

112. George W. Bush (Republican) was President of the US between 2001 and 2009.

113. Gordon Brown (Labour) was UK Prime Minister between 2007 and 2010.

114. Deborah Summers, "Brown steps in after Digby Jones calls for half of civil service to be sacked," *The Guardian*, 15 January 2009.

115. Robert Huggins and Nicholas Williams, "Enterprise and Public Policy: A Review of Labour Government Intervention in the United Kingdom" (*Environment and Planning C: Politics and Space, Volume: 27 issue: 1*): 19-41.

116. Gordon Brown speech in 2010

117. Barack Obama (Democrat) was President of the US between 2009 and 2017.

118. David Cameron (Conservative, Prime Minister) and Nick Clegg (Liberal Democrat, Deputy Prime Minister) formed a coalition government following the 2010 general election which had resulted in a hung parliament. The Conservative Party won the 2015 election with a majority, so Cameron remained UK Prime Minister until 2016.

119. Speech by Chancellor George Osborne to close his 2011 Budget Statement setting out the government's aspirations.

120. Speech at the launch of Start Up Britain on 28 March 2011.

121. Theresa May (Conservative) became the UK Prime Minister in 2016 and remains in office at the time of publication.

122. *"Business formations fall after tax clampdown,"* Centre for Entrepreneurs, January 2018.

123. Peter Evans, "Theresa May blamed for fall in number of start-ups," *The Times*, January 28, 2018.

124. See BBC online 15 to 17 September 2018.

125. Donald Trump (Republican) became President of the US in 2017 and is in office at the time of publication.

126. See NFIB Small Business Optimism Index, 11 September 2018.

127. Number of new business start-ups (less than one year old) in 2015: 679,072. In 1994 this was 569,419 (Source: Bureau of Labor Statistics, https://www.bls.gov/bdm/entrepreneurship/entrepreneurship.htm)

128. Number of jobs created by US companies less than one year old was 4.1 million in 1994 but 3 million in 2015. Number of new jobs in each new establishment is declining (Source: Bureau of Labor Statistics).

129. In the last ten years, the lowest survival rate was 45.4% for establishments started in 2006, and a high of 51.0% for those started in 2011.

130. The period 1993 – 2006 was marked by a high level of business 'churn' with greater numbers of businesses closing and starting up. The start of the recession in 2007 resulted in a marked drop in start-ups. From 2008 – 2010, there were more business closures than start-ups recorded (Source: Bureau of Labor Statistics).

131. Rand Fishkin, *Lost and Founder. A Painfully Honest Field Guide to the Startup World* (London: Penguin Random House UK, 2018), 5.

132. Anonymous, Start-up Business Demography Dataset 2011-2016, Office of National Statistics, 21 November 2017.

133. Anonymous, *Financing growth in innovative firms: consultation*, (London, HM Treasury, 2017), 20.

134. See Kishore Mahbubani, *The Great Convergence. Asia, the West and the Logic of One World* (New York: Public Affairs, 2013), 1.

135. Kishore Mahbubani, *The Great Convergence. Asia, the West and the Logic of One World* (New York: Public Affairs, 2013), 195.

136. Kishore Mahbubani, *The Great Convergence. Asia, the West and the Logic of One World* (New York: Public Affairs, 2013), 47.

137. Kishore Mahbubani, *The Great Convergence. Asia, the West and the Logic of One World* (New York: Public Affairs, 2013), 33.

138. Kishore Mahbubani, *The Great Convergence. Asia, the West and the Logic of One World* (New York: Public Affairs, 2013), 3.

139. Deng Xiaoping was Paramount Leader of the Chinese Communist Party between 1978 and 1992.

140. Anonymous. *Experience Gained in the Development of China's Special Economic Zones* (Washington DC: World Bank Group, 2015).

141. Ziyang, Zhao. "Advance along the road of socialism with Chinese Characteristics – Report delivered at the 13th National Congress of the Communist Party of China on October 25, 1987." In *Beijing Review*, Volume 30, No 45.

142. Chang, Gene Hsin. "Macroeconomic issues and policies." In *Dilemmas of Reform in Jiang Zemin's China*. Andrew Nathan, Zhaohui Hong (ed). Boulder, CO: Lynne Rienner, 1999, 161.

143. Li, Huaqun. "History and Development of Entrepreneurship in China." In *Entrepreneurship and Economic Growth in China*. Ting Zhang and Roger Stough. Singapore: World Scientific, 22.

144. Yudkin, Marcia. "Making Good – Private Business in Socialist China." *Beijing Review*, November 9-15, 1987. 19.

145. Kahn, Joseph. "China's Communist Party, 'to Survive', Opens Its Doors to Capitalists." *The New York Times*, 4 November 2002.

146. Nathan, Andrew. "Introduction: Dilemmas of Development." In *Dilemmas of Reform in Jiang Zemin's China*. Andrew Nathan, Zhaohui Hong (ed). Boulder, CO: Lynne Rienner, 1999, 5.

147. Naughton, Barry. "Deng Xiaoping: The Economist." *The China Quarterly* No. 135, Special Issue: Deng Xiaoping: An Assessment (Sep., 1993), pp. 491-514.

148. Anonymous. "The Second Long March." *The Economist*, 11 December 2008.

149. For discussion of societal implications of enterprise policy see Evan Osnos, *Age of Ambition, Chasing Fortune, Truth and Faith in The New China* (London: Penguin Random House, 2014), 62, 150.

150. Jiang Zemin was Paramount Leader of the CPC between 1992 and 2002.

151. Li, Huaqun. "History and Development of Entrepreneurship in China." In *Entrepreneurship and Economic Growth in China*. Ting Zhang and Roger Stough (ed). Singapore: World Scientific. 22

152. Wu, Guoguang. "Legitimacy Crisis, Political Economy, and the Fifteenth Party Congress." In *Dilemmas of Reform in Jiang Zemin's China*. Andrew Nathan, Zhaohui Hong (ed). Boulder, CO: Lynne Rienner, 1999, 21.

153. Wu, Jinglian and Quian, Yingyi. "Working Paper no 69: China's Transition to a Market Economy: How Far Across the River?" Stanford University Center for Research on Economic Development and Policy Reform September, 2000.

154. For discussion of societal implications of enterprise policy see *Evan Osnos, Age of Ambition, Chasing Fortune, Truth and Faith in The New China* (London: Penguin Random House, 2014), 7, 62, 150.

155. Anonymous, "The Redistribution of Hope," *The Economist*, 16 December 2010. See article for research regarding global optimism.

156. Kishore Mahbubani, *The Great Convergence. Asia, the West and the Logic of One World* (New York: Public Affairs, 2013), 23.

157. Cited in Kishore Mahbubani, *The Great Convergence. Asia, the West and the Logic of One World* (New York: Public Affairs, 2013), 171.

158. Panagariya, Arvind. "India in the 1980s and 1990s: A Triumph of Reforms." (New York: World Bank, 2004), 7.

159. Anonymous. "Can India work? India's economic reforms." *The Economist*, 10 June 10 2004.

160. India Code: Digital Repository of all central and State Acts. "Thee Micro, Small and Medium Enterprises Development Act, 2006."

161. Burke, Jason. "Narendra Modi's landslide victory shatters Congress's grip on India." *The Guardian*, 16 May 2014.

162. Anonymous. "Prime Minister Narendra Modi starts up new business era with tax breaks and mega fund." *The Times of India* 17 January 2016.

163. Anonymous. "India's prime minister is not as much as a reformer as he seems." *The Economist* 24 Jun 2017.

164. World Bank. *Doing Business 2017: Equal Opportunity for All.* Washington, DC: World Bank. DOI: 10.1596/978-1-4648-0948-4.26.

165. Government of India. "About Stand up India". Accessed 11 October 2018. https://www.standupmitra.in/Home/AboutUs

166. Government of India. "About Start-up India". Accessed 11 October 2018. https://goa.start-upindia.gov.in/content/sih/en/start-upgov/about-us.html

167. Singh, Suman. "IMF retains India's GDP growth forecast for FY19 at 7.3%, cuts global growth forecast for 2018 to 3.7%." *CNBC*, 10 October 2018.

168. Government of India. *All India report of Sixth Economic Census.* New Delhi: Government of India. https://msme.gov.in/sites/default/files/All%20India%20Report%20of%20Sixth%20Economic%20Census.pdf.

169. Statistic generated between 1993 and 2004. See Gupta, Vipin. "An Inquiry into the Characteristics of Entrepreneurship in India." *Journal of International Business Research* Vol 7 No 1. (Special issue 1, 2008).

170. Kishore Mahbubani, *The Great Convergence. Asia, the West and the Logic of One World* (New York: Public Affairs, 2013), 29, 30.

171. Gupta, Vipin. "An Inquiry into the Characteristics of Entrepreneurship in India." *Journal of International Business Research* Vol 7 No 1 (March 2008).

172. McKinsey and Company. "India's economy: Why the time for growth is now." September 2016.

173. For discussion see Wharton University of Pennsylvania. "Has the 'Dream Run' for Indian IT ended?" 14 April 2017.

174. See Digby Jones, *Fixing Business: Making Profitable Business Work For The Good Of All* (UK: John Wiley & Sons, 2017).

175. Abacus, An Imprint of Little, Brown Book Group, 2017.

176. Evan Davis, *Post-truth. Peak Bullshit And What We Can Do About It* (London: Abacus, 2018) 177.

177. For further discussion of this point see Linda Yueh, *The Great Economists. How Their Ideas Can Help Us Today* (London: Viking an imprint of Penguin Books, 2018) 21.

178. Linda Yueh, *The Great Economists. How Their Ideas Can Help Us Today* (London: Viking an imprint of Penguin Books, 2018) 3.

179. Linda Yueh, *The Great Economists. How Their Ideas Can Help Us Today* (London: Viking an imprint of Penguin Books, 2018) 3.

180. Mariana Mazzucato, *The Entrepreneurial State. Debunking Public versus Private Sector Myths* (London: Penguin Random House UK, 2018) 52.

181. Hsieh and Klenow cited in Mariana Mazzucato, *The Entrepreneurial State. Debunking Public versus Private Sector Myths* (London: Penguin Random House UK, 2018) 52.

182. His book *Great to Excellent: It's in the Execution!* is a quick but powerful read. If you get the chance to hear him speak, seize it.

183. As detailed in Jim Alampi, *Great to Excellent; It's in the Execution! Overcoming the Natural Barriers to Profitable Company Growth* (Jim Alampi, 2013). See www.alampi.com and www.theexecutionmaximizer.com to source a copy.

184. Gartner, William B., "'Who is an Entrepreneur?' is the Wrong Question" University of Illinois at Urbana-Champaign's Academy for Entrepreneurial Leadership Historical Research Reference in Entrepreneurship (1988).

185. See Viktor E. Frankl, *The Will to Meaning. Foundations and Applications of Logotherapy*, (New York: PLUME Penguin Group, expanded edition, 2014) 3.

186. See Viktor E. Frankl, *The Will to Meaning. Foundations and Applications of Logotherapy* (New York: PLUME Penguin Group, expanded edition, 2014) 120.

187. Carl Rogers, *On becoming a person: A therapist's view of psychotherapy* (London: Constable, 1961).

188. Evan Davis, *Post-Truth. Peak Bullshit And What We Can Do About It* (London: Abacus, an imprint of Little, Brown Book Group, 2017) 65, 275.

189. See Evan Davis, *Post-Truth. Peak Bullshit And What We Can Do About It* (London: Abacus, an imprint of Little, Brown Book Group, 2017) 296.

190. Perhaps a better question is not why do you perpetuate a harmful Myth, but why wouldn't you want to be considered a superhero? Humility is a rare characteristic. Perpetuating your own myth may well make psychoanalytical sense – in the short term.

191. Nicolson, L. (2001) 'Modelling The Evolution Of Entrepreneurial Mythology'.

192. See Howard Sail Becker, *Outsiders: Studies in the Sociology of Deviance*. (New York: The Free Press, 1973).

193. Evan Davis, *Post-Truth. Peak Bullshit And What We Can Do About It* (London: Abacus, an imprint of Little, Brown Book Group, 2017) 19.

194. Rand Fishkin, *Lost and Founder. A Painfully Honest Field Guide To The Startup World* (London: Penguin Random House UK, 2018) 7, 204.

195. Smith, M. (2013). Anti-stigma campaigns: Time to change. *British Journal of Psychiatry, 202*(S55), S49-S50.

196. Nicolson, L. (2001) 'Modelling The Evolution Of Entrepreneurial Mythology'.

197. The ultimate rallying cry for instinctive thinking and snap judgements is Malcolm Gladwell, *Blink: The Power of Thinking Without Thinking* (London: Penguin Books, 2005).

198. Shelley Davidow and Paul Williams, *Fail Brilliantly. Exploding the Myths of failure and Success* (US: Familius Books, 2017) 78, 42, 48.

199. Mark Earls, *Herd. How to Change Mass Behaviour By Harnessing Our True Nature* (Chichester, West Sussex: John Wiley & Sons, 2009).

200. Mark Earls, *Herd. How to Change Mass Behaviour By Harnessing Our True Nature* (Chichester, West Sussex: John Wiley & Sons, 2009) 106 -108.

201. Ruef, Martin. *The Entrepreneurial Group: Social Identities, Relations, and Collective Action.* Princeton, NJ: Princeton University Press, 2010, 15- 16.

202. See Ruef, M. 2010. *The entrepreneurial group: social identity, relations, and collective action.* Princeton University Press.

203. See Ucbasaran, Deniz, Lockeet, Andy, Wright, Mike, Westhead, Paul. "Entrepreneurial Founder Teams: Factors Associated with Member Entry and Exit". *Entrepreneurship: Theory and Practice* Vol 28, no 2 (Winter 2002).

204. Kamm, J., Shuman, J., Seeger, J., & Nurick, A. "Entrepreneurial Teams in New Venture Creation: A Research Agenda" *Entrepreneurship Theory and Practice*, Vol 14 No 4 (Summer 1990) 7-17.

205. See James Surowiecki, *The Wisdom of Crowds. Why the Many are Smarter than the Few* (London: Abacus, 2005). Also, Mark Earls, *Herd* (West Sussex: John Wiley and sons, 2009). Also, Rachel Botsman and Roo Rogers, *What's Mine is Yours. How Collaborative Consumption is Changing the Way We Live* (London: Collins. An Imprint of HarperCollinsPublishers, 2011).

206. See the pithy commentary on leadership loneliness: Rose Cartolari, 'It's Lonely At The Top', *Forbes.com*, 18 October 2017. Listen also to the BBC podcast: Evan Davis The Bottom Line, episode 'Lonely at the Top?' bbc.co.uk/sounds/play/b0739rfv

207. All quotes in this paragraph from Robert B. Reich "Entrepreneurship Reconsidered: The Team as Hero." *Harvard Business Review* 65 (May 1987). 77 – 83. Essential reading and a vivid call to team entrepreneurship.

208. For a useful literature review, see Lucia Crevani et al, "Shared Leadership: A Postheroic Perspective on Leadership as a Collective Construction" *International Journal of Leadership Studies* Vol.3 Issue.1, (2007), pp40-67. See also, Alex Stewart, Team Entrepreneurship (Newbury Park: Sage Publications, 1989).

209. Lucia Crevani et al, "Shared Leadership: A Postheroic Perspective on Leadership as a Collective Construction".

210. See www.ted.com/talks/rachel_botsman_the_case_for_collaborative_consumption and Rachel Botsman and Roo Rogers, *What's Mine is Yours. How Collaborative Consumption is Changing the Way We Live* (London: Collins. An Imprint of HarperCollinsPublishers, 2011) 68.

211. Mariana Mazzucato, *The Entrepreneurial State. Debunking Public versus Private Sector Myths* (London: Penguin Random House UK, 2018) 53.

212. Michael Bhaskar, *Curation. The Power of Selection in a World of Excess* (London: Piatkus, 2017) 54-60.

213. Michael Bhaskar, *Curation. The Power of Selection in a World of Excess* (London: Piatkus, 2017) 49.

214. James Reason, *The Human Contribution. Unsafe Acts, Accidents and Heroic Recoveries.* (Farnham, Surrey: Ashgate Publishing, 2008) 101.

215. James Reason, *The Human Contribution. Unsafe Acts, Accidents and Heroic Recoveries* (Farnham, Surrey: Ashgate Publishing, 2008) 3, 37.

216. James Reason, *The Human Contribution. Unsafe Acts, Accidents and Heroic Recoveries* (Farnham, Surrey: Ashgate Publishing, 2008) 240.

217. See James Reason, *The Human Contribution. Unsafe Acts, Accidents and Heroic Recoveries* (Farnham, Surrey: Ashgate Publishing, 2008).

218. See Juan-Carlos Ayala and Guadalupe Manzano, "The Resilience of the Entrepreneur. Influence on the Success of the Business. A Longitudinal Analysis." *Journal of Economic Psychology*, Vol.42, June 2014, p126-135. See also Amanda Bullough and Maija Renko, "Entrepreneurial Resilience during Challenging Times." *Business Horizons*, Vol.56. Issue.3, May-June 2013, p343-350.

219. Quoted in Stefan Cantore and Jonathan Passmore, *Top Business Psychology Models. 50 transforming ideas for leaders, consultants and coaches* (London: Kogan Page, 2013) 92.

220. See Stefan Cantore and Jonathan Passmore, *Top Business Psychology Models. 50 transforming ideas for leaders, consultants and coaches* (London: Kogan Page, 2013) 66 for discussion on psychological capital.

221. See Luthans et al, "The Development and Resulting Performance Impact of Positive Psychological Capital" *Human Resources Development Quarterly*, Vol.21 (1), 2010, 41-67. Also, Luthans et al, "Positive Psychological Capital: measurement and Relationship with Performance and Satisfaction" *Personnel Psychology*, Vol.60 (3), 2007, 541-72.